THE NEW YORK METS

The 1986 World Champions, with some of their fans.

THE NEW YORK METS

THE FIRST QUARTER CENTURY

DONALD HONIG

WORLD SERIES CHAMPIONSHIP EDITION

CROWN PUBLISHERS, INC.
NEW YORK

The years mentioned in parentheses in the picture captions indicate years the player spent with the Mets.

Published by Crown Publishers, Inc., 225 Park Avenue South, New York, New York 10003 and represented in Canada by the Canadian MANDA Group.
This book was previously published in different form as *The New York Mets Official 25th Anniversary Book.*

CROWN is a trademark of Crown Publishers, Inc.

Manufactured in the United States of America

Library of Congress Cataloging-in-Publication Data

Honig, Donald.
The New York Mets.

Includes index.
1. New York Mets (Baseball team)—History. I. Title.
GV875.N45H66   1987   796.357′64′097471   87-15585
ISBN 0-517-56604-4

10 9 8 7 6 5 4 3 2 1

First Revised Edition

For Andrew Aronstein

CONTENTS

ACKNOWLEDGMENTS

THE METS NOT ONLY HAVE A FINE TEAM on the field, they have another one in their front office. This book could not have been written without the help of these willing, able, patient, and highly spirited people. I would like particularly to thank the following: Al Harazin, Michael Aronin, Jay Horwitz, Tim Hamilton, James Plummer, Maryanne Gugliotto, and most especially the Mets' staff photographer Dennis Burke, much of whose brilliant work appears in this book.

I would like to thank the following sources for permission to use their photographs: *Sports Illustrated* and their talented photographers Ronald C. Modra, Anthony Neste, John Iacono and Chuck Solomon for the color photographs that follow page 116; Wide World Photos for the photographs on pages 151–158; Neal Boenzi and New York Times Pictures for the frontispiece photograph (page ii).

Thanks also to Dennis D'Agostino, whose book *This Day in New York Mets History* was an invaluable source. Further thanks are offered to the following for their wise counsel: Stanley Honig, David Markson, Lawrence Ritter, Michael Aronstein, Andrew Aronstein, Mary Gallagher Mulcahy, Allan J. Grotheer, Thomas Brookman, Donna Cornell of the National Baseball Hall of Fame and Museum library at Cooperstown, and last but not least to my always encouraging editor Pamela Thomas.

THE NEW YORK METS

Studying a model of the stadium-to-be are three men who played critical roles in bringing National League baseball back to New York. *Left to right:* Branch Rickey, Mayor Robert F. Wagner, and William Shea.

1
A NEW TEAM IN TOWN

THE SEEDS THAT WERE TO BECOME the New York Mets were planted in 1957, the year the Brooklyn Dodgers and New York Giants heeded a venerable American siren call and headed west in search of gold and greater glory. Suddenly New York City was without National League representation. Not just one club, but two had drawn roots and departed, leaving behind their fans and their history and their traditions, and leaving behind Ebbets Field and the Polo Grounds, those old ball parks that were part of the lives of every fan.

Incredibly, the National League was to remain without a team in New York for four years. When one realizes that today much smaller and less vital cities like Seattle and Kansas City have major-league teams, it drives the imagination to extremities to think of New York without a National League club. Equally as extraordinary is the fact that the league made no effort of its own to fill this vacuum. The eight other club owners were content to accept their own purblind vision of reality and forgo the revenue, the prestige, and the overall stimuli that derives from having a team in the cultural and communications heart of the nation.

New York City, however, was not content to sit idly by forever. In the fall of 1957, Mayor Robert F. Wagner established a committee of four prominent New Yorkers to explore the possibility of bringing the city back into the league it had been part of since 1883. The four were Clint Blume, Bernard Gimbel (of department store fame), former Postmaster General James A. Farley, and a young attorney named William Shea. Of the four, Shea proved to be the most active.

Along with brains, initiative, and determination, William Shea brought to his task two other assets: he was a genuine sports fan, and he was quietly active in Democratic politics. As a close friend of the powerful Mayor Wagner, Shea had clout.

Shea's first move was to try to entice another National League club to New York. He approached the owners of the Cincinnati, Pittsburgh, and Philadelphia franchises. After expressing some initial interest, the Reds and Pirates backed off. The Phillies gave Shea an outright refusal.

The next route available to Shea was to get the League to expand from eight teams to ten, with one of the expansion clubs being a new New York National League entry.

This idea made a lot of sense. Major-league baseball had been a sixteen-club monopoly since the turn of the century. That was now two world wars ago, before radio, television, the automobile, the airplane. Towns had grown to cities in that time and certain of those cities had begun petitioning for major-league baseball. Some changes had already taken place—Baltimore had acquired the St. Louis Browns, Milwaukee the Boston Braves, Kansas City the Philadelphia Athletics, San Francisco the New York Giants, and Los Angeles the Brooklyn Dodgers. Those, however, had been one-for-one translocations, and there were still just sixteen major-league teams.

The sixteen big-league owners turned frozen faces upon the idea of expansion. True monopolists, they refused to share. The face of the future, however, belonged to William Shea, and the wily, determined lawyer refused to be deterred.

If no existing National League club would come to New York, if the league remained adamantly opposed to expansion, then Shea saw only one other course: create a third league.

It was a bold idea; it was shrewd and imaginative. One way or another, Shea reasoned, it would get results.

In order to bring credibility to the concept of a third league—the Continental League—Shea enlisted the services and the prestige of Branch Rickey. In 1959 Rickey was seventy-eight years old, but he had lost none of the acuity that for decades had made him baseball's reigning intellectual and most daring innovator. He was the man who had conceived and developed baseball's farm system, and in 1947 he had defied his colleagues in baseball's front-office suites by bringing Jackie Robinson to the major leagues and thus leaving the game's odious color barrier broken and unmendable.

With well-heeled businessmen and combines in cities around the country ready to back new franchises, Shea and Rickey had no trouble lining up outposts for their new league. The eight cities selected were New York, Houston, Toronto, Minneapolis–St. Paul, Denver, Buffalo, Dallas–Fort Worth, and Atlanta. (That six of the eight are now part of major-league baseball is an indication of the foresight of Shea and Rickey.)

The thought of a third league was enough to revive some old nightmares for the baseball establishment. In 1901, when the American League muscled itself into existence, there had been pirating of players, broken contracts, expensive litigation, fulminations, recriminations, and, finally, grudging peace. In 1914, a confection known as the Federal League had come swirling out of the dust, proclaimed itself a major league, and begun offering scandalous sums of money to established players to induce them to jump the line. The Federal League had died of inertia after two years, but it had been an expensive two years for the two established leagues who had had to hike many salaries in order to keep their employees from departing.

Although there was a lot of convincing talk about the Continental League, much of it was simply that—talk. What Shea was really after was expansion, the most sensible and least troublesome solution. He was certain that the major-league structure would yield to the chimeras evoked by the threat of a third league.

Baseball had long enjoyed a special status conferred by Congress that exempted it from anti-trust regulations. But if baseball tried to obstruct or otherwise interfere with a bona fide new enterprise—like a third league—the foundation of that special status might become shaky. The specter of the Continental League was William Shea's wedge to pry apart the sealed doors of major-league baseball and force it to expand.

While major-league baseball fumed and fret-ted, Shea and Rickey moved forward with plans for a third league. Formal organization was effected on July 27, 1959, with Rickey as president. The target date for play to begin was April 1961.

When Congress failed to pass a law overturning baseball's favored antitrust status, the Continental League seemed doomed. But the talk, the controversy, and the mere thought of having had their cherished status challenged had been enough to change the thinking of the establishment. Moving quickly to take advantage of this vacillation, Shea announced on August 2, 1960, that if four of its proposed franchises were absorbed into the major leagues (two in each league), the Continental League would dissolve itself.

On October 16, 1960, National League club owners met in Chicago to vote on the question of expansion. A resolution to make the first structural change in the league since 1900 was unanimously passed. The National League would expand to ten teams, with New York and Houston being the new members. According to league president Warren Giles, the addition of the two new teams was a "giant progressive step toward bringing major-league baseball to all four corners of the country."

When William Shea had been making noises about the Continental League and New York's representation in it, he found some very willing backers for the team. They included Mrs. Charles Shipman Payson, the former Joan Whitney of the affluent, socially prominent Whitneys. (The family enterprises included, among other things, the New York *Herald Tribune*.) Initially one of several investors in the team, Mrs. Payson soon bought out her partners and emerged as the largest single stockholder, owning about 80 percent of the club soon to become known as the New York Mets. (The nickname was adapted from the formal handle given the team as an entry for the Continental League: the New York Metropolitan Baseball Club, Inc.)

In Joan Payson the Mets had a vivid personality in the executive suite. In many respects she was a true blueblood. She was a patron of the arts, active in charitable causes, involved in the betterment of civic institutions, a generous donor to hospitals and the advancement of medicine. Together with her brother Jock Whitney, she owned Greentree Stables, a stable of blooded racehorses.

Joan Payson had come into the world abundantly gifted. One gift, however, she cultivated on her own: the human touch. The engaging personality that was to infuse the Mets from the very outset began with their owner. This well-bred millionaire society matron was comfortably at home sitting behind her team's dugout eating peanuts and hot dogs and rooting for her heroes with the uninhibited fervor of the average fan.

Her interest in baseball was enthusiastic and genuine. Originally a New York Giants fan, she had been a minority stockholder in that team and had tried in vain to talk owner Horace Stoneham out of moving the Giants to San Francisco, even offering to buy the team in order to keep them in New York. When William Shea asked her if she was interested in investing in a brand-new major-league club for New York, she said yes. Her initial investment was around $4 million.

Once she had assumed ownership of the team, Mrs. Payson immediately reverted to the status of fan, appointing a board of directors to run the club. Chief among these was M. Donald Grant. Grant was a Wall Street financier and close associate of Mrs. Payson's. He was also a longtime baseball fan. It was Grant, in fact, who as a minority stockholder and board-of-directors member of the Giants had cast the lone dissenting vote against the team's move to San Francisco.

It was now the fall of 1960. New York had been assured of renewed representation in the National League. The team had owners, a board of directors, a suite of offices, a name, and little else. What was missing was pretty substantial: players, a manager, a baseball-wise general manager, and a place to play.

George Weiss (*left*) and Mrs. Joan Payson.

Casey Stengel.

Casey, outnumbered by an employer and a wife. Mrs. Payson *(center)* and Edna Stengel.

The Polo Grounds, home of the Mets during their first two years.

Catcher Hobie Landrith, the Mets' first choice in the expansion draft. Hobie played in New York for just a few weeks before being traded to Baltimore for Marv Throneberry.

Clarence ("Choo Choo") Coleman (1962–63, 1966). Said Mr. Stengel of Mr. Coleman: "A great scooper of pitches in the dirt."

Roger Craig (1962–63).

Richie Ashburn joined the Mets in 1962 after fourteen years as one of the National League's premier outfielders. He played in New York for just one season, became the Mets' first .300 hitter when he batted .306, then retired to become a broadcaster.

Elio Chacon (1962). Elio was the shortstop for much of the Mets' first season, batting .236.

Left-hander Alvin Jackson (1962–65, 1968–69), one of the Mets' better pitchers in their struggling early days. His 13 wins and 142 strikeouts in 1963 were club records broken by Tom Seaver in 1967.

Bob ("Righty") Miller (1962, 1973–74). Bob was just 1–12 in 1962, but thereafter had a fine career as a relief pitcher, working in all for ten major-league teams before returning to the Mets to end his career in 1974.

Right-hander Craig Anderson (1962–64).

Chris Cannizzaro (1962–65). Stengel never got it right, calling him "Canzoneri." But under any name, Chris was an excellent catcher, batting .311 as a part-time worker in 1964.

Frank Thomas (1962–64), one of the genuine boppers of the early days. In 1962 he hit 34 home runs and drove in 94 runs.

Don Zimmer (1962), the Mets' first third baseman. He played just 14 games and was then traded to Cincinnati, leaving behind an .077 batting average. Some people feel the position has never recovered.

Jim Hickman (1962–66). One of the steadier men in the Mets outfield, Jim hit 17 homers in 1963.

Gil Hodges (1962–63, Manager 1968–71). Injuries limited Gil's playing time with the Mets. In 1962 he got into just **54** games and batted .252.

THE OPENING YEARS

ON OCTOBER 13, 1960, THE BASEBALL season came to a sudden and resounding conclusion when Pittsburgh's Bill Mazeroski belted a home run in the bottom of the ninth inning of the seventh game of the World Series to give the Pirates the championship. The blow not only closed out a season, but also ended an era in baseball.

The team the Pirates defeated was the New York Yankees, winners of ten pennants in twelve years under their seventy-year-old manager Casey Stengel. A few days later the Yankees surprised the baseball world with the announcement that under the team policy regarding employees at age sixty-five, Stengel was "retiring." No one had ever heard of this policy before, and with good reason—it had not existed before. Stengel had been fired and the old wisecracker was not shy about letting the world know it. Despite twelve years of unprecedented success, Casey had begun to grate on his employers and on certain of his players. So baseball's most famous manager and one of its most recognizable names was out of work.

Several weeks after discharging Stengel, the Yankees slipped the rug out from under their general manager, George Weiss. Weiss, who had been with the club for decades, was one of the acknowledged architects of Yankee success. First as farm director and later as G.M., the cold and unsentimental Weiss had helped build and sustain a Yankee machine of unparalleled efficiency.

Stengel and Weiss were two extremely dissimilar personalities. Stengel was folksy, witty, spontaneous; but at the same time he was as shrewd and wily a baseball lifer as had ever laced up a spiked shoe. He had traveled every conceivable baseball byway since before World War I, as player, coach, manager, minor-league executive. To the public he was an ageless Huck Finn, an amiable con man willing to play the clown when it suited his needs. But to those on the inside he was

a hard-as-flint student of the game with a baseball intellect that was as deep as his memory was long.

Of George Weiss it was said—paraphrasing Will Rogers—that he never met a man who liked him. But this frosty baseball executive had his own goals and standards and as long as he kept attaining them he didn't seem to much care whether he was liked or not. As much as anyone, George Weiss seemed the guardian and personification of the then Yankee image—cold, businesslike, remorselessly efficient. His players found him ruthless in contract negotiations and many despised him. But no one ever doubted the acumen he brought to the front office.

In one of the more unlikely baseball matchings, Weiss and Stengel had a long friendship that stretched back to the 1920s when both were affiliated with minor-league teams in the Eastern League. Their mutual respect was deep and sincere. In 1949, when Stengel was the surprise choice to take over as Yankee skipper, it was at the behest of General Manager Weiss, who had had to convince his employers that the gnarled old veteran with the craggy face and fanned-out ears was hardly the clown the newspapers liked to depict.

So suddenly in the fall of 1960 this improbable duo were out of work. In March 1961, in what was to be one of many moves to bring a New York coloration to the club, the Mets hired Weiss as general manager, although his official designation was club president. (When Weiss had left the Yankees it was with a lucrative five-year retirement package, with the stipulation that he not work as general manager for any other club. By making Weiss president, the Mets had finessed the arrangement. The Yankees merely growled and looked the other way.)

Instead of building from the ground up, the natural way, the Mets were building from the top down, the only way they could. They now had a president who was in effect a general manager. After hiring some scouts and administrative personnel, Weiss began trying to nail down his manager.

As far as George Weiss was concerned, there was only one man for the job as first manager of the New York Mets—Casey Stengel. Casey had been a winner for a dozen years in New York, he had a great relationship with the press, was one of the most widely known names in sports, and, despite his age, was still hale of body and sharp of mind.

It took some persuasian to bring Stengel back into the game. He had already turned down the managerial job of the Detroit Tigers. But by the end of the 1961 season—the first he had spent outside of professional baseball since 1909—the seventy-two-year-old baseball junkie had become restless. On September 29, the Mets confirmed what had become a pretty hot rumor: Charles Dillon ("Casey") Stengel would be managing the Mets when they took the field for the first time in 1962.

And where would that field be? Well, it would be in upper Manhattan and would be a very familiar place—the old Polo Grounds, home of John McGraw, Christy Mathewson, Mel Ott, Bill Terry, Carl Hubbell, Willie Mays, and many others. Abandoned since the Giants' departure, the horseshoe-shaped old ball park would be home to the Mets until they could build a home of their own.

The new ball park, the first in New York City since Yankee Stadium opened in 1923, was to be built in Flushing Meadow in Queens with money raised through a bond issue that had been authorized by the state legislature. The Flushing site made Queens the fourth of five New York City boroughs to have a big-league club, following Manhattan (the Giants), the Bronx (the Yankees), and Brooklyn (the Dodgers). But until the new stadium could be built—an estimated two years— the Mets would play their home games in the venerable, peculiarly shaped place Stengel called "the Polar Grounds." For Stengel there was probably a bit of nostalgia in nearly every ball yard in the country, but few offered the old boy as much sentiment as the Polo Grounds. It was here that he played the outfield for his managerial idol, McGraw, in the early 1920s, the declining years of

his journeyman's career, when he was beginning to think of managing as a second career.

Now it was time for the final step to be taken, the one most intriguing to those old Dodger and Giant stalwarts who were taking things on faith and declaring themselves Mets fans—the selection of a team.

The Mets (and the similarly brand-new Houston club) had pushed, bluffed, and connived their way into the National League, but now that they were in they were going to have to play by the rules, rules set up by the league.

The formula presented for stocking the new teams was this: Each of the eight existing National League teams would establish a player pool for the new clubs to draw from by making available fifteen players for selection, seven from their twenty-five-man roster and eight whose contracts they owned in the minor leagues. The new teams were required to take two players each from each team at $75,000 apiece. After that, if they so desired, the new clubs could each take one more player from every established team for a price of $50,000 per man. When these selections were complete, there would be made available a "premium" player—one per club—with a $125,000 price tag. New York and Houston were entitled to four each of these players.

The outlay for players would cost the new teams close to $2 million apiece, a rather expensive ticket of admission into major-league baseball.

The expansion draft took place on October 10, 1961, in Cincinnati. By that good old scientific method, the coin toss, Houston won the right to select first. They chose shortstop Eddie Bressoud of the San Francisco Giants. The Mets' first pick was another Giant, catcher Hobie Landrith. Stengel explained the choice with impeccable logic: "Without a catcher you'll have a lot of passed balls."

And then piece by piece the team—the Original Mets—was put together. For $75,000 each, the Mets selected the following:

Pitchers: Roger Craig (from Los Angeles), Al Jackson (Pittsburgh), Craig Anderson (St. Louis), and Ray Daviault (San Francisco).

Catchers: Landrith, Chris Cannizzaro (St. Louis), and Clarence ("Choo-Choo") Coleman (Philadelphia).

Infielders: Gil Hodges (Los Angeles) and Ed Bouchee (Chicago), first basemen. Other infielders were Elio Chacon (Cincinnati), Felix Mantilla (Milwaukee), and Sammy Drake (Chicago).

Outfielders: Gus Bell (Cincinnati), Joe Christopher (Pittsburgh), Bobby Gene Smith (Philadelphia), and Johnny Demerit (Milwaukee).

At the more accommodating $50,000 price, the Mets selected outfielder Jim Hickman from Chicago and pitcher Sherman ("Roadblock") Jones from Cincinnati.

The final phase of the draft involved the so-called premium players, four of them to be selected by each club for the price of $125,000 apiece. The Mets selected two pitchers, right-handers Jay Hook from Cincinnati and Bob Miller from St. Louis; outfielder Lee Walls from Philadelphia, and infielder Don Zimmer from Chicago.

At the end of the session the Mets were poorer by $1,800,000, but through the expenditure twenty-two ballplayers had materialized, giving physical substance to the entity known as the New York Mets.

Of course what the Mets had selected was hardly an all-star team. The National League clubs had not been expected to dispose of any choice talent, nor had they. Of the twenty-two players, there were only three "names." Gil Hodges had had a great career in Brooklyn and Los Angeles, but was now thirty-seven years old; at age thirty-three, Gus Bell's prime years were behind him; and Roger Craig, once one of the Dodgers' most effective starters, was coming off a 5–6 year in 1961 after having broken his shoulder in 1960.

What Weiss was trying to do was filter into his team enough veteran players to give it some semblance of "big league." Hodges, Craig, and Zimmer also helped bring a bit of Brooklyn familiarity to the club. Soon after the draft, Weiss obtained another former Brooklyn Dodger, second baseman Charlie Neal, in a swap with the Dodgers for Lee Walls. And before the year was out, Weiss added slugger Frank Thomas from Milwaukee and Richie Ashburn from Chicago, both outfielders. These were two veterans with considerable mileage on them, but also with some good baseball left in them.

In late October ground-breaking ceremonies had taken place for the stadium that was to rise at Flushing Meadow. The team was hoping it would be ready for the 1963 season, but as it developed, the Mets were going to have to wait until 1964 to break the seal on their new home.

Soon there were other announcements of great importance to a modern big-league operation. In mid-November, WOR-TV (Channel 9 in New York City) obtained the rights to televise the Mets games. Hired to announce the games were three men who would go on to establish a remarkable record for longevity in their jobs. They were Lindsey Nelson, a cheerful, unflappable veteran of college football broadcasts as well as NBC's "Game of the Week" baseball telecasts; Bob Murphy, a sharp and able professional with nine years of experience in the booth at Boston and Baltimore; and Pittsburgh's former home-run king, Ralph Kiner.

And of course there was that priceless public-relations asset, the manager himself—Mr. Stengel. Casey had no illusions about his new club. The old man had been around too long to have illusions about anything. Somewhere along the line he had already located the spirit and character of his new charges by calling them "amazin'." This was before the club had even been assembled, much less played their first game. But Stengel the irrepressible phrasemaker had tossed off one destined for long and affectionate usage. Through the years, as their exploits ran the gamut from the unlikely to the extraordinary, the appellation "Amazin's" would prove adaptable to every contingency, and for the New York Mets the contingencies were going to be many and varied.

Jay Hook (1962–64), winner of the first Mets game, after the club had dropped its first nine in 1962.

Outfielder Joe Christopher (1962–65). Joe's best year was 1964, when he hit 16 home runs and batted .300.

First baseman Ed Bouchee (1962). After some productive seasons with the Phillies and Cubs, Ed put in his final big-league year with the Mets.

Felix Mantilla (1962), who played shortstop for the Mets in their first game. Felix batted .275 and hit 11 homers, then was traded to the Red Sox.

Charlie Neal (1962–63). Charlie batted .260 in 1962, then was traded to Cincinnati the following year.

Announcer Bob Murphy, with the Mets from the beginning.

Ralph Kiner, an original member of the Mets' broadcasting team, one of the greatest home-run hitters in baseball history, and a Hall of Famer.

The third of the original Mets announcers, Lindsey Nelson left the Mets in 1979 to call the games for the San Francisco Giants.

Casey entertaining the press during spring training at St. Petersburg, Florida, in March 1963.

Cliff Cook (1962–63). Another early candidate for third base.

Catcher Harry Chiti (1962), the man who was traded for himself.

Marv Throneberry. Marvelous Marv.

This one isn't Throneberry's fault. He's going up for a throw that's high and wide as the Cardinals' Bob Gibson hustles for the base. The coach is Harry Walker. The action took place on July 1, 1962, at the Polo Grounds.

CASEY AND THE AMAZIN'S

THE METS TOOK THEIR FIRST SPRING training at St. Petersburg, Florida. As Stengel sent his troops through their drills under the hot Florida sun, he and Weiss fine-tuned the roster and prepared to field a starting lineup for Opening Day in St. Louis on April 10.

The Mets won a few exhibition games—12 of 27, to be exact—and this made for encouraging reading back home. But Casey wasn't fooled. The skipper had a knowing eye for talent; he also had an equally discerning eye for lack of it. But Stengel was too much the quipster and P.R. man to show his dismay. He promised nothing except that it was going to be "a rousin' season." If at times he felt like a candidate for martyrdom, he kept it to himself, or at least off the record.

But no manager has ever come closer to volunteering for the martyr's role. Strengel could have stayed retired; he certainly was wealthy enough, and surely he was old enough. He could have sat home in Glendale, California, secure in the pride of his Yankee years—ten pennants in twelve years. But he didn't, because he was first and last a baseball man, and a loyal friend, and when Weiss appealed to him, Casey responded on both accounts. And in so doing he became the alchemist who began mixing and brewing the curious, captivating elixir that was to become the Mets legend. No one expected a miracle from this team, nor did one occur. What did occur was the wildly and wonderfully unexpected, which some might say bears certain kinship with the miraculous.

After Opening Day in St. Louis was rained out ("That was their first victory," one whimsical Mets fan noted later), Stengel's boys took the field for the first time in earnest on April 11, 1962. That first starting lineup read as follows:

Ashburn, cf	Thomas, lf	Zimmer, 3b
Mantilla, ss	Bell, rf	Landrith, c
Neal, 2b	Hodges, 1b	Craig, p

This would have been a most capable club in its prime, but behind most of these players was a considerable passage of seasons that came under the heading of "best years."

Gus Bell's second-inning single was the first Mets hit, while Gil Hodges's fourth-inning home run the first round-tripper. But the truer pattern was set in the final score: Cardinals 11, Mets 4.

Nevertheless, the Mets arrived in New York the next day and were treated to a ticker-tape parade and City Hall reception. The Yankees must have been jolted into the reality that they were suddenly sharing the city with something instantaneously magical. After all, the 1961 Yankees had set an all-time home record with 240 one-way tickets, topped by Roger Maris's record 61 and Mickey Mantle's 54. The Yankees had, in addition to these two lusty bangers, galahads like Yogi Berra, Elston Howard, Bill Skowron, Tony Kubek, Bobby Richardson, and Whitey Ford. The Yankees were world champions. But the parade went to the Mets, lifetime record 0–1.

Stengel's intrepid orphans and castoffs opened the season the next day—Friday the 13th, no less—at the Polo Grounds, overseen by the bemused ghosts of John McGraw and Christy Mathewson. Just 12,447 fans (soon to be dubbed "The New Breed") showed up on a chilly day. They watched the new giant in town lose a close one to Pittsburgh, 4–3, the sort of defeat that was to become a moral victory throughout the long, long summer that lay ahead.

It wasn't until April 23, after nine straight losses, that Jay Hook pitched the club to its first win, a 9–1 bruising of the Pirates. The euphoria lasted just one day as the Mets journeyed to Cincinnati and saw their "winning streak" brought to an end by the Reds. Nevertheless, one Mets fan could exult, "We took one in a row." This spirit was telling. The brand-new team had begun shaping a tradition of defeat and disaster that would, paradoxically, prove to be priceless and make its later triumphs appear cosmic.

There were occasional bursts of glory. On April 28 the Mets slugged five home runs in an 8–6 win over the Phillies—two by Neal, one each by Hodges, Thomas, and Hickman. For the struggling young club this was an explosion of near-seismic proportions.

But the indelible image of the 1962 Mets was of a club fighting to rise from futility to mediocrity. One of the more imagination-catching nonfeats of the season was Don Zimmer's 0-for-34 slump, which he broke on May 4 with a two-bagger. Moving while Zim was hot, the Mets a few days later traded him to Cincinnati for infielder Cliff Cook and pitcher Bob Miller. The trade fit in neatly with the club's developing character, for it now gave them two Bob Millers, both pitchers. The first Bob Miller was a right-hander, the new one a left-hander. They soon became known as Bob "Righty" and Bob "Lefty."

On June 15 the Mets sent catcher Harry Chiti to Cleveland. This was a transaction of little moment, except that on April 26 they had obtained Chiti from Cleveland for a player to be named later. Two months later Harry became that player, meaning the net effect of the transaction was that Harry Chiti was traded for himself.

But it was on May 9 that the Mets made one of their most fortuitous deals, in a manner of speaking. It was not a trade destined to elevate them in the standings nor improve by much their daily efforts. What the Mets had inadvertently achieved in this bit of trafficking was the acquisition of a player who for the moment would prove more precious than hits or runs, for like it or not, the Mets were developing and embellishing a collective personality laced with the kind of wit, charm, and human fallibility that is seldom associated with any team in any sport, much less a losing one. The man they acquired on May 9 was soon to become the lovable symbol of all the things the Mets were and all the things they were not.

His name was Marv Throneberry, soon to become known as "Marvelous Marv," a nickname applied with affectionate facetiousness. He was obtained from the Baltimore Orioles in exchange for Hobie Landrith.

Throneberry had originally come to the big leagues with Stengel's Yankees. The big, strong, left-handed-hitting first baseman had rung up some impressive minor-league slugging credentials, something that made the Throneberry persona even more interesting—when Marv laid into one he could send it a long way. The Yankees liked him and thought he had a future. But Marv never made it in the stadium, batting .227 in 1958 and .240 in 1959. He played in Kansas City in 1960, then was swapped to Baltimore in mid-season 1961.

Now he was back in New York, reunited with Stengel, and destined to become a folk hero of sorts, with a second career as a personality in television commercials awaiting him, commercials that traded with good-natured jocularity on the Throneberry "legend." But in 1962, Marv was a strong, serious, big-league first baseman struggling to make good. He was going to be given the chance, too, because Hodges was suffering with a bad knee that was rapidly forcing his long career to an end.

Marv tried his best. But his best never quite cut the mustard, but rather left it splattered here and there. He was slow afoot and not exceedingly mobile afield. He blundered and he lumbered, and occasionally he popped a long one—16 home runs in little more than half a season's work. He also hit three triples and by rights had earned two more, but they were never recorded, thanks to some overzealous footwork.

It is the quintessential Throneberry story. Twice he ripped long line drives into the Polo Grounds' deep acreage, and each time he was called out for failing to touch second base. The second time, Stengel came charging out of the dugout to protest the injustice, but before he could cross the white lines Casey was intercepted by coach Cookie Lavagetto.

"Forget it, Case," Cookie said. "He didn't touch first either."

One never quite knew from day to day what new adventure this team might unveil. On May 20 they swept a doubleheader from Milwaukee and then immediately plunged into a 17-game losing streak. On June 30 they were victimized by a Sandy Koufax no-hitter. And in consecutive games on August 1, 2, and 3, Frank Thomas belted six home runs, two per game, tying a record set by Mets announcer Ralph Kiner. On August 14 the slightly built left-hander Al Jackson pitched all 15 innings in a 3–1 loss to the Phillies, in the process throwing an unbelievable 215 pitches.

And so it went, down to season's end. On September 30 they lost their 120th and final game, the most ever by a major-league club in the twentieth century.

Forty wins and 120 losses as forty-five players came and went during the course of the season. Outside of Frank Thomas's 34 homers and Richie Ashburn's .306 batting average, there wasn't much to cheer by way of individual performance. Stengel's "big three," who started 100 games among them, logged the following records: Craig, 10–24; Hook, 8–19; Jackson, 8–20. Craig Anderson was 3–17, while Bob "Righty" Miller posted a 1–12 record.

But, remarkably enough, something very positive had happened. The original Mets had made a most crucial contribution by establishing a team persona. The team had won the hearts and affection of a city, a city purportedly inhospitable to losers, but a city sophisticated enough to see not dreariness or buffoonery in the team's performance but rather an almost Chaplinesque quality. If they were perceived as clowns, then it was as clowns in the classic sense, with identifiable and empathic human traits, with an exaggerated ritual for defeat, of enduring travails with a certain endearing charm. Invariably opposed by greater talent, they were noble in victory, heroic in defeat.

When last seen in New York, National League baseball had been the powerful if aging Brooklyn Dodgers and a drab New York Giants. New York baseball had been the monopoly of the monotonously successful Yankees. Unreconstructed National League fans in New York still rooted wistfully for Willie Mays in San Francisco and for "the Brooklyns" in Los Angeles. But they were, in fact, fans without a team.

Now, however, they had a team, and New York had never seen anything like them, not since the "Daffy Dodgers" of the 1920s anyway. Baseball is a game of passing seasons and transient names, so it wasn't just Stengel and Choo-Choo Coleman and "Hot Rod" Kanehl and Marvelous Marv. These pioneers were soon gone, but what remained and continued to be sustained was an aura, and not solely an aura of lovable losers, but

the limning of an image, the materializing of a baseball team that people had drawn close to.

The proof was at the box office. In their first year of play the Mets drew to the antiquated Polo Grounds 922,000 customers, in the process outdrawing Milwaukee, Chicago, and Philadelphia, and holding even with the new Houston club. They had proved something that was astonishing and perhaps unique in professional sports—losing does not necessarily have to be dismal or unprofitable.

The 1963 roster showed some significant changes. Marv Throneberry, most memorable of the early Mets, was replaced at first base by Tim Harkness, whom the Mets acquired from the Dodgers along with second baseman Larry Burright in a trade for Bob "Righty" Miller, who went on to become a crack reliever for the Dodgers. Burright was soon replaced at second by a hard-nosed kid named Ron Hunt, a scrapper and a hustler who had a knack for getting clipped with pitches. (In his twelve-year career, the first four spent with the Mets, he set a record by getting plunked 243 times, including a record 50 times with Montreal in 1971.) In 1964 Hunt would become the first Met to start in an All-Star Game.

At shortstop the Mets had Al Moran, a dazzling fielder with a weak bat. Playing first base and outfield was eighteen-year-old Ed Kranepool, a big, handsome bonus baby from James Monroe High School in the Bronx. It was the beginning of an eighteen-year Mets career for Kranepool, a longevity record for the club. Purchased from the Braves was a hard-throwing right-hander named Carlton Willey.

On April 1, just before the start of the season, the Mets made a "nostalgia" deal that warmed the hearts of many of their fans when they purchased Duke Snider from the Dodgers. At the age of thirty-six, the former "Duke of Flatbush" was near the end of an illustrious career. He played just one year for the Mets, batting .243 and hitting 14 home runs, including the 400th of his career.

The 1963 season opened with a case of *déjà vu* for Mets fans. The team lost its first eight games. This was a slightly better opening than they had in their maiden season when they dropped their first nine games, but only the most sublime optimist could find a ray of hope in that.

Actually, the Mets did post an improved record over the year before, winning 51 and losing 111, finishing 48 games out of first place, a "climb" of 12½. The pitching staff trimmed its earned-run average by nearly a full run—down to 4.12 from 5.04. The hitting, however, fell off precipitously, from .240 to .219. Ron Hunt's .272 topped the regulars.

The season's high for merriment came on July 23 when Jimmy Piersall, purchased from Washington a month earlier, hit his 100th career homer and celebrated the occasion by running the bases backward. (The pitcher who was stung by this historic blow was Philadelphia right-hander Dallas Green, later manager of the Phillies and general manager of the Cubs. Dallas also pitched briefly for the Mets in 1966.)

The season's standard for gloom, misery, and hard luck was set by Roger Craig. The tall right-hander, a truly fine pitcher, suffered through an 18-game losing streak that was finally snapped on August 9 thanks to a grand-slam homer by Jim Hickman. Craig, who was traded to the Cardinals that fall, had a record of 5–22 in 1963 despite a very respectable 3.78 earned-run average. The philosophical North Carolinian said in later years that the extreme adversity he endured as a Met helped him to build character. With a two-year Mets record of 15–46, including many late-inning heartbreakers, Craig must have emerged from the ordeal with a bit more character than he needed.

And through it all Stengel never lost his sense of the theatrical. His "Amazin' Mets," he said, were coming up with ways of losing he had never known existed. For instance, what happened on the night of August 27 in Pittsburgh. The Mets were leading 1–0 in the bottom of the ninth. Galen Cisco was pitching. There was one out. Cisco walked Dick Schofield. The next batter, Manny Mota, hit a ground ball. It might have been a game-ending double play, and end the game it did, but this was how:

Cisco put his glove down, but the ball skipped by. Shortstop Al Moran and second baseman Ron Hunt tried to surround it, but the ball slipped through and kept going into center field. Center fielder Duke Carmel charged in, but the ball bounced over his glove. But right fielder Joe Christopher was right on the job, backing up.

Schofield, meanwhile, was rounding third, while Mota was on his way to second. Pitcher Cisco was backing up third. Christopher's peg sailed in a vague direction somewhere between third and home. Trying to run it down, Cisco tripped and fell. Schofield was home with the tying run. Cisco got up and ran after the ball, which had caromed far behind home plate. Mota was rounding third and barreling home with the winning run. When Cisco picked up the ball he had Mota cold—except that catcher Jesse Gonder was standing with his back to the plate waiting for Cisco's throw. When Jesse received the throw and whirled to make the tag he discovered that he was located about five feet from the dish, five feet from the incoming Mota, who slid home with the winning run as Gonder was putting the tag on thin air.

Stengel, with fifty years of baseball behind him, stood in the dugout dumbfounded. Even he had never seen one like this before.

Nevertheless. There was a new chant to be heard in New York: "Let's Go Mets!" It could be excited or affectionate or facetious. But it was always there, a hearty rallying cry. No matter what blunders or mistakes were taking place down on the field, the Mets had been accepted with full embrace, like some endearing, long-lost, ne'er-do-well relative who suddenly reappears, with a quip and a wink of the eye.

Undismayed by another tenth-place finish, "The New Breed" were out stronger than before in 1963, spinning the turnstiles to a final count of 1,080,000. The 111-game losers, the .219 hitters, had outdrawn Milwaukee, Chicago, Cincinnati, Houston, Philadelphia, and Pittsburgh.

"My Amazin' Mets," Stengel never tired of saying. "They're amazin'."

So were their fans.

The Mets' improvement in 1964 was so slight as to make little difference. In their third year of play they finished at 53–109 and 40 games behind. After having had six pitchers lose in double figures the year before, the 1964 staff for the first time had three double-figure winners—Al Jackson at 11–16, newcomer Jack Fisher 10–17, and right-hander Tracy Stallard, 10–20. Both former American Leaguers, the two right-handers had been engraved on the trivia lists by Roger Maris in 1961: Fisher had thrown number 60 to Roger

Rod ("Hot Rod") Kanehl (1962–64), who won a lot of fans with his spirited play. A versatile man, Rod played every position for the Mets except pitcher and catcher. The best he could muster at the plate, however, was .248 in 1962.

Left-hander Ken MacKenzie (1962–63), the only Mets pitcher with a winning record in the early days—5–4 in 1962, 3–1 in 1963, when he was traded to the Cardinals. When the Yale-educated pitcher mentioned to Stengel that he had the lowest salary of anyone in his graduating class, the skipper reportedly replied, "Yes, but the highest earned-run average."

An old Brooklyn Dodgers reunion at the Polo Grounds on Opening Day, 1962. *Left to right:* Don Zimmer, Clem Labine, the recently retired Don Newcombe, and Charlie Neal. Labine pitched in just a few games for the Mets before being released.

and Stallard the record-breaking number 61. (Fisher, a young man with a knack for crashing the history books, had also coughed up Ted Williams's dramatic final home run in 1960.)

The Mets jumped their team batting average 27 points to .246. The main contributors were Ron Hunt at .303 and Joe Christopher at an even .300.

There were some memorable occasions during the Mets' 1964 season, and they took place in a brand-new home—Shea Stadium (named for William Shea, the energetic and resourceful lawyer who had helped godfather the club into existence).

Shea Stadium opened on April 17, 1964. The first game ever in the new park saw the Mets lose to the Pirates 4–3, but as in so many Mets games of that era, the final score was only part of the story. What was most significant here, for both the team and their fans, was the psychological boost received from having, at last, their own home.

The Flushing Meadow home of the New York Mets was and is an almost perfect ball park. That bane of modern baseball—the artificial surface—does not deface this ball park; in Shea Stadium baseball is played on real grass, as God and man intended it to be. The sight lines are unobstructed by pillars. The outfield dimensions are reasonable and equitable, allowing for neither immodest home runs nor extravagant fly outs. It is 338 feet down each line, 371 in the power alleys, and 410 to straightaway center.

Shea Stadium was first and foremost built for baseball, and six weeks after it opened, the new ball yard was given a memorable shakedown cruise, Mets style.

The date was May 31. This was the day of the endless doubleheader between the Mets and Willie Mays's San Francisco Giants. With a smashing crowd of 57,037 on hand, official business got under way at 1 P.M. The first game was as normal and uneventful as a ball game could be—Juan Marichal and the Giants glided to a standard-brand 5–3 victory. The second game was the whopper, the lalapalooza, the breaker and maker of records. It took all of 7 hours and 23 minutes for the Giants to defeat the Mets in 23 innings, 8–6.

What the *New York Times* called "monumental endurance records" included the following:

Longest game in time elapsed in major-league history: 7 hours, 23 minutes.

Longest doubleheader in history: 9 hours 52 minutes of playing time. (Those fans who came out for batting practice and stayed to the bitter end were in the ball park for about 12 hours.)

Most innings played in one day: 32.

In addition, twelve pitchers racked up new strikeout records—36 in one game and 47 in one day. For good measure, the Mets pulled off a triple play in the 14th inning, and Willie Mays put in some time at shortstop.

With the Mets losing 6–3 in the bottom of the seventh, Joe Christopher hit a game-tying three-run homer. After that came 15 scoreless innings until the Giants finally scored two runs in the top of the 23rd on a pinch double by Del Crandall and an infield hit by Jesus Alou. When the Mets' Amado Samuel made the final out in the bottom of the 23rd, it was 11:25 P.M.

A month after this herculean doubleheader, Philadelphia's Jim Bunning provided Shea fans with the direct opposite—the slickest, most seamless performance a pitcher can deliver. On June 22, the tall sidewheeling right-hander fired a perfect game against the Mets, the first in the National League since 1880. When Bunning, working in 91-degree heat, fanned pinch-hitter John Stephenson for the final out, over 30,000 fans rose and gave him an ovation.

This was the first game of a doubleheader, and these were the days when the Mets were setting records for futility. In losing the second game 8–2, the Amazin's managed just three hits. That total, three hits in a doubleheader, tied a major-league record for offensive anemia.

So again it had been a losing season, but once again the fans had demonstrated their allegiance with a socko attendance of 1,732,000. This figure was topped by only one other club in the major leagues—the Los Angeles Dodgers. This meant that in just their third year of existence the Mets were the second-largest draw in baseball. Their attendance exceeded that of the pennant-winning Yankees by more than 400,000.

Pennant winners the Yankees were, for the fifth straight year. But right after the World Series the Yankees stunned everyone by firing their manager, Yogi Berra. Quick to pick up an available glamor name, the Mets on November 17 signed

Berra as a player-coach. (Yogi was more coach than player, however, batting just nine times before taking himself off the roster.)

The enchantment of the Mets continued in 1965. Despite another tenth-place finish, the club's 1,768,000 paid admissions topped every major-league club with the exceptions of the Dodgers and the Houston Astros (who opened their Astrodome that year).

It was not a very good year for the team nor for individual performances. On the mound, Al Jackson was 8–20, and Jack Fisher, despite a 3.93 ERA and many fine efforts, was 8–24. No other pitcher won as many as eight games. The rest of the team had almost uniformly dismal years. The twenty-year-old Kranepool, installed as the club's first baseman, led the regulars with a .253 batting average. The Mets got some superlative defense from veteran shortstop Roy McMillan, and they received some unexpected power from twenty-one-year-old rookie outfielder Ron Swoboda, who hit 19 home runs. In the bullpen that year was a young left-hander named Tug McGraw, and breaking into a few games with no noticeable impact were two other youngsters—shortstop Buddy Harrelson and outfielder Cleon Jones.

As usual, the Mets couldn't let a season go by without playing a game or two out of the ordinary. On June 14, Cincinnati's hard-throwing right-hander Jim Maloney was positively awesome, holding the Mets hitless for 10 innings while both teams went scoreless. In the top of the 11th, however, the Mets' Johnny Lewis hit a home run and the New Yorkers went on to a 1–0 victory. Making Maloney's losing effort even more impressive were his 18 strikeouts, a record for whiffs in an extra-inning game.

On October 2, the Mets participated in another odd one. After being shut out in the first game of a doubleheader by Philadelphia's Jim Bunning, the Mets played the Phillies to an 18-inning 0–0 tie that was finally called by a 1 A.M. curfew. The Phillies' Chris Short and the Mets' Rob Gardner dueled for the first 15 innings, with Short fanning 18 to equal the record for strikeouts in an extra-inning game set by Maloney against the Mets in June.

The following day the Mets finished the season with another doubleheader against the Phillies, losing by scores of 3–1 and 3–1 in 13 innings. So they had closed out their season by scoring 2 runs in their last 49 innings.

The big news of 1965, however, was the retirement of Casey Stengel. The Mets management had for some time been wondering what to do about their seventy-five-year-old skipper. It had become painfully apparent to many that Casey no longer possessed either the physical stamina or mental alertness needed to run a major-league team. There were mutterings from some of his players that the old boy was falling asleep on the bench during games, that he would conduct rambling, irrelevant monologues during games, and that sometimes he simply did not seem to know or care what was going on.

The Mets hierarchy weren't quite sure what to do about their legendary manager. They appreciated what Casey had done for their fledgling team. But if the Mets were finally going to build themselves into contenders it was going to have to be done with young players, and if Stengel had a weakness it was in developing a rapport with young players.

Stengel, however, gave no indication of wanting to do anything but go on and on. It was becoming a highly delicate and somewhat uncomfortable situation.

Then, on July 24, fate lent a hand, or gave a push. Sunday, July 25, was to be Old-Timers' Day at Shea Stadium. On Saturday the 24th, there was a party for the visiting celebrities at Toots Shor's restaurant. During the evening, Casey stumbled and fell hard. X-rays taken the next morning confirmed a fracture of the left hip. Despite some brave and optimistic proclamations from his hospital bed, Casey Stengel's big-league career, which had begun in 1912, was over. It was five days before his seventy-fifth birthday.

On August 30, Casey made it official: he was stepping down. His successor was Wes Westrum, a coach who had been running the club as interim manager in Stengel's absence.

Stengel remained in the Mets organization, was given a title of vice president and charged with some very vaguely defined scouting responsibilities in California. He was a consultant during spring training, a good man to have on a dais, and as always, a splendid force to turn loose on the media.

Westrum, who had joined the club as a coach in 1965, was another familiar face from New York's baseball past. He had caught for the Giants for eleven years and been the bulwark behind the plate during the 1951 "Miracle" season that culminated in Bobby Thomson's be-all and end-all home run in the playoffs against the Dodgers. Never much of a hitter for average, Wes did swing with power, but was best known as a fine defensive catcher. He was forty-three years old in 1965 and the Mets were his first big-league managing assignment.

The sizable age disparity was not the only difference between the new manager and the old. Westrum, a likable and unpretentious man, had none of his predecessor's wit, eccentricity, or lack of inhibition. Wes was a serious, solid, and capable professional. If he lacked Stengel's zany unpredictability, well, maybe it was time for a change.

Though no one could possibly have known it at the time, despite their fourth straight tenth-place finish, some rays of light were beginning to permeate the darkness. The club liked the way young Cleon Jones swung the bat, and they liked the range, quickness, and instincts shown by young Bud Harrelson at shortstop. And on October 19 the Mets acquired twenty-three-year-old catcher Jerry Grote from Houston in exchange for Pitcher Tom Parsons. It was to prove one of the most significant deals in Mets history.

The first breezes of the exhilarating hurricane that was to come had begun blowing across Shea Stadium.

Roger Craig has just missed getting his man at first base. Throneberry is whirling to get the umpire's call.

Galen Cisco (1962–65), a right-hander who pitched well in a losing cause in the Mets' early years.

First baseman Tim Harkness (1963–64).

Ron Hunt (1963–66). The popular, hard-nosed second baseman batted .303 in 1964 and that year became the first Mets player to start in an All-Star Game.

Second baseman Larry Burright (1963–64).

Al Moran (1963–64), one of the slickest of shortstops, but unfortunately too light of stick.

Shea Stadium in 1963, still under construction.

Ed Kranepool, who saw it all from 1962 through 1979.

Carlton Willey (1963–65). The hard-throwing right-hander won nine games in 1963, four of them shutouts.

Catcher Jesse Gonder (1963–65). Jesse could hit—.304 in 1963, .270 the next year—but his catching sometimes left something to be desired.

The colorful Jimmy Piersall. He was with the Mets for part of the 1963 season, long enough to hit his 100th career homer, run the bases backward, and then depart.

Right-hander Larry Bearnarth (1963–66). Larry did some fine relief work for the Mets until a sore arm ended his career when he was just twenty-five years old.

Stengel with two great veterans of the Brooklyn wars, Gil Hodges (left), and Duke Snider. Snider was with the Mets for just one year (1963), batting .243 with 14 home runs.

Al Jackson.

Jack Fisher (1964–67). The workhorse right-hander was one of the Mets' top pitchers, but his four-year record in New York of 38–73 shows he was up against it. In 1965 he was 8–24.

One of the greatest fielding shortstops of all time, Roy McMillan (1964–66) closed out his career with the Mets.

Tracy Stallard (1963–64), another pitcher who pitched some good ball in losing causes in the Mets' early days. He was a 20-game loser in 1964 despite a 3.79 earned-run average.

Charley Smith (1964–65). The Mets' regular third base-man for a while, Charley could hit with power—20 home runs in 1964, 16 the next year.

George Altman (1964). George, a solid hitter with the Cubs and Cardinals for five years, batted just .230 for the Mets, then was traded on to the Cubs.

An aerial view of a packed house at Shea. The stadium opened in 1964.

Bob ("Hawk") Taylor (1964–67), reserve catcher.

Bobby Klaus (1964–65), utility infielder.

Casey Stengel explaining the ground rules to the umpires and Cardinals Manager Red Schoendienst.

Frank Lary (1964–65). Detroit's former ace right-hander tried to crank it up for the Mets after suffering a sore arm, but never quite made it back.

Casey Stengel and Donald Grant being serenaded by an accordion player.

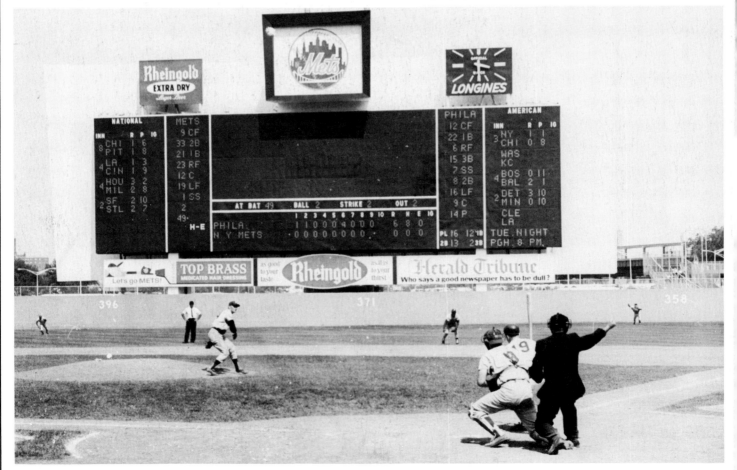

The scoreboard tells the story. It's the last pitch of Jim Bunning's perfect game at Shea on June 22, 1964. Pinch-hitter John Stephenson has just swung and missed at Bunning's final, history-making pitch.

Second baseman Chuck Hiller (1965–67). Chuck batted .280 as a part-timer in 1966, leading the league with 15 pinch hits.

Johnny Lewis (1965–67). The left-handed-hitting outfielder hit 15 home runs for the Mets in 1965.

Spring training 1966 finds three Mets outfielders obliging the cameraman. *Left to right:* Jim Hickman, Ron Swoboda, and Cleon Jones.

Frank ("Tug") McGraw (1965–74). One of the finest relief pitchers in Mets history, and one of the team's most colorful characters.

Warren Spahn (1965). The winningest left-hander in baseball history (363) spent part of his twenty-first and last big-league season with the Mets. The forty-four-year-old lefty was 4–12 before moving on to the Giants.

Twenty-year-old shortstop Bud Harrelson in 1965. With the Mets from 1965 through 1977, he remains the club's all-time shortstop.

Wes Westrum, Mets manager (1965–67).

The man who got away: Nolan Ryan (1966, 1968–71).

THE PRE-MIRACLE YEARS

IN 1965 THE CHICAGO CUBS FINISHED eighth. Soon after, they hired a new manager, Leo Durocher. One of the first things Leo offered all interested parties was this assurance: "I can guarantee you one thing: the Cubs won't finish eighth again." The 1966 season proved Leo correct: the Cubs did not finish eighth. They finished tenth and last. That tenth spot had for four years been the exclusive preserve of the New York Mets. So where did the Mets go? After going 4-for-4 in last place, the Mets had relinquished their basement apartment. The elevator didn't travel far, only up one notch to ninth place.

"It's a step in the right direction," said one Mets fan.

"It was a step in the only direction," responded another.

Glacial progress, maybe. But progress.

Under the quiet, self-effacing Westrum, the Mets ran off a 66–95 record, the best in their brief history and good enough to nudge them up that one spot in the standings. And as the Mets enjoyed increased prosperity on the field, so did they at the turnstiles as their fans came thronging in record numbers—over 1,932,000 of them.

Ron Hunt led the regulars with a .288 batting average, while utility infielder Chuck Hiller batted .280. Cleon Jones, an outfield fixture now, hit .275 in his first full season. Ed Kranepool's 16 home runs led the team. But as an indication of how weak the club's attack still was, the team RBI leader was veteran third baseman Ken Boyer with 61. (Boyer, one of the great third basemen in National League history, had been obtained from the Cardinals the previous fall in a deal that saw Al Jackson head west.)

On the mound, the Mets showed three 11-game winners in right-handers Dennis Ribant (11–9), Bob Shaw (11–10), and Jack Fisher (11–14). A nineteen-year-old righty with breathtaking speed named Nolan Ryan made his big-league debut,

pitching three innings and, significantly, fanning six. The quiet young Texan had launched what was to become baseball's all-time strikeout career.

When the veteran shortstop McMillan suffered an injury late in the season, Harrelson was installed at the position. So Buddy was there to stay now, and Jones was in left field, and Grote was catching. Kranepool and Swoboda were playing regularly, and McGraw was in the bullpen and getting better. Quietly, things were beginning to fall into place.

But the most important thing to happen in 1966, and, as far as player personnel is concerned, perhaps the most crucial event in club history, took place just before the opening of the season. On February 24, the Atlanta Braves signed a twenty-one-year-old right-hander named George Thomas Seaver. A native Californian and ex-Marine, Seaver was then a student at the University of Southern California. Believing they had hauled in a prize catch, the Braves enriched the personable young man with a $50,000 bonus.

The Braves had indeed netted a prize, one destined to become one of the greatest of pitchers. Wittingly or not, however, the Atlanta club had committed what amounted to a technical infraction of a recently adopted rule. In order to assure the integrity of college baseball, the rule provided that a college player in his junior or senior year was off-limits to organized ball once his season had started. The Braves had signed Seaver after the commencement of the USC season.

When the infraction was brought to the attention of Commissioner William Eckert, the commissioner was compelled to act. His determination was that a rule was a rule and that it clearly had been broken. Consequently, Eckert nullified Seaver's contract with the Braves and declared the young pitcher a free agent. Under the commissioner's ruling, any club was free to deal with Tom, as long as they guaranteed him a bonus equal to what the Braves had paid. If more than one club expressed interest, then by that venerable scientific method of drawing a name from a hat would the matter be settled.

Only three teams showed interest—the Cleveland Indians, Philadelphia Phillies, and New York Mets. Accordingly, on April 2, 1966, Commissioner Eckert wrote the names of those teams on slips of paper, dropped them into a hat, closed his eyes, and drew one out. The slip read METS. And thus from this chancy, "luck of the draw" procedure was the future of the Mets to become so dramatically altered.

The following day the Mets signed Seaver for a bonus of $50,000 and sent him to Jacksonville, Florida, of the International League. It would be his one and only year of minor-league ball. Pitching at one level beneath the big leagues, Seaver logged a 12–12 record, not terribly impressive until one took a closer look: 188 strikeouts and just 66 bases on balls in 210 innings. The word from all who saw him pitch that summer was, actually, two words: "can't miss."

So, not realizing that destiny had begun edging in their direction, the Mets labored through their 1966 season, scratching toward their moral triumph of ninth place. In July that year they had the most successful month in their history with an 18–12 record.

There was a major change in the front office after the season. The club's original architect, George Weiss, retired. His replacement as the club's number one decision maker was Vaughan ("Bing") Devine. Devine was a St. Louis product who had worked his way up from avid Cardinal fan to the club's general manager, with years of administrative training in the Cardinal farm system along the way. A man of sound judgment when it came to evaluating talent, the forty-eight-year-old Devine had built the Cardinals' 1964 championship team via trades that enhanced the team with the likes of Curt Flood, Dick Groat, Lou Brock, Bill White, and other star performers.

Devine, who had joined the Mets in 1964 as Weiss's top assistant, lost no time in exercising his mandate. Two weeks after taking over, he traded the popular Ron Hunt and Jim Hickman (Hickman was the last of the 1961 expansion draftees still with the Mets) to the Dodgers for outfielder Tommy Davis, a former two-time batting champion, and infielder Darrell Griffith. A week later the new G.M. sent pitcher Dennis Ribant and outfielder Gary Kolb to the Pirates for outfielder Don Bosch and pitcher Don Cardwell. The key man in this deal as far as the Mets were concerned was Bosch, whom the club believed would settle their center-field problems. Bosch, however, never made it. Cardwell, on the other hand, was an experienced major-league pitcher who gave the Mets three years of capable work.

On February 10, 1967, Devine made what would turn out to be a most salutary purchase when he bought relief right-hander Ron Taylor from Houston's Oklahoma City farm team. Another weaver of the upcoming "Miracle" was now in place.

But in spite of everyone's best efforts, 1967 proved to be a disappointing year for the Mets. Perhaps the purer air of ninth place had been too rarefied; but whatever the reason, the Mets sank back into the last spot with a 61–101 record. (If there was any solace in this, it was that their won-lost record was the second best in club history.) Adding to the discomfort of last place was a nearly 400,000 drop-off in attendance. The million and a half they pulled was still impressive (only three teams in baseball outdrew them, and they continued to outdraw the Yankees), but the falloff was something to be concerned about.

It wasn't that the Mets didn't try in 1967. Like a safecracker playing with combinations, they used a league-record fifty-four players that summer, twenty-seven of them pitchers (also a league record). Despite all the shuffling, there were quite a few fixtures—Kranepool at first, Harrelson at short, Ed Charles (an early-season pickup from Kansas City) at third, Grote behind the plate, and Jones, Swoboda, and Tommy Davis in the outfield. Davis, a man with a line-drive bat, led the regulars with a .302 batting average.

On the mound, the Mets unveiled the young man who became that year their first Rookie of the Year, Tom Seaver. The twenty-two-year-old with the cuddly good looks, infectious giggle, smoking fastball, flawless pitch, and keen intelligence, rang up an impressive freshman season. Pitching for a .238-hitting, 101-game loser, Seaver was 16–13, setting a team record for wins. He also set club records with 170 strikeouts, 18 complete games, and a 2.76 earned-run average.

Behind Tom on the mound was Jack Fisher, struggling gamely to a 9–18 record. The next top winner was Cardwell, just 5–9, but a much more effective pitcher than that showed. Ron Taylor was the top gun in the bullpen, with fifty appearances and a 2.34 ERA. Among the many other pitchers who came and went that season was a twenty-four-year-old hard-throwing left-hander, Jerry Koosman. The Minnesota farmboy got into just nine games, with an 0–2 record and 6.14 ERA. But the Mets liked his fastball, a whistler that broke in on the hands of right-handed batters.

One of the problems, among many facing the club, was lack of an "identifying" personality. In the beginning, Stengel and old hands like Hodges and Snider had been able to provide a bit of big-league presence and status, as well as a nostalgic link to better days. The club now lacked this. Though affable, competent, and well liked, the serious-minded Westrum lacked "color." Unlike Stengel, he could not deflect defeat with quips and diverting monologues. Seaver was still a rookie, and Davis, the squad's top hitter, was not the sort of personality to excite the crowds. The young players, promoted as the heralds of a brighter future, had thus far been quiet disappointments. Kranepool batted .269 in 1967, Grote .195, Jones .246, Harrelson .254. The only "name" on the club was Yogi Berra, and he was a coach.

Nor was there a virtuoso of lovable ineptitude like Throneberry, nor would one have been tolerated any longer. The team was six years out of the chute now. The fans had proved their loyalty, they had enjoyed the show. But now they were beginning to wonder if, and when, there would be a better show. Somewhat wistfully, they had watched as the Boston Red Sox rose from a ninth-place finish in 1966, went through an "Impossible Dream" year, and won the American League pennant in 1967.

So in the deadweight gloom that accompanies a season of failed expectations and falling attendance, Wes Westrum showed both his sense of reality and his pride. On September 21, with a handful of games still on the schedule, the skipper handed in his resignation. Coach Salty Parker ran the club for the final 11 games.

There was little debate among the Mets hier-archy about the man they wanted to replace Westrum. He was the current manager of the Washington Senators, Gil Hodges.

Hodges had left the Mets in 1963 to take over the new Washington Senators (the old Washington club had moved to Minnesota in 1961 when the American League expanded to ten teams.) For five years Hodges had struggled in the American League's lower depths with his team, with a sixth-place finish in 1967 his best showing. Nevertheless, he had proven himself a skilled and patient manager and was highly valued by his employers.

Washington was reluctant to let their skipper go, but after the Mets obtained permission to talk to him it soon became evident that Hodges wanted the job. The Indiana-born strongboy had played first base for the Brooklyn Dodgers from 1948 through 1957 and in that time had sunk roots in Brooklyn, where he still lived. The slugging, smooth-fielding first baseman had been a particular favorite of Dodger fans, a genuinely beloved figure. For Hodges it would be a home-coming, for Mets fans a familiar, comfortable figure, and for the Mets a perfect choice.

Beyond his extraordinary athletic abilities, Hodges had been known for two other things—his soft-spokenness and his remarkable physical strength. The gentleness of his nature made the strength the more intimidating. There was something about this quiet man that evoked respect, even caution. A Gil Hodges–run team was serious and businesslike; there was no rule breaking, no defiance of the manager. "He managed by intimidation," one of his players said.

On October 11, in the midst of the Red Sox–Cardinals World Series, the Mets announced the appointment of their new manager. (In order to pry Hodges loose from Washington, the Mets sent pitcher Bill Denehy and a pile of cash reported to be around $100,000.) The club gave Hodges a three-year contract. In signing Hodges, the Mets were continuing the old New York connection. Their managers had thus far been the ex-Yankee Stengel, the ex-Giant Westrum, and now the ex-Dodger Hodges.

Soon after, on December 5, 1967, Bing Devine resigned to return to his former club, the Cardinals, as general manager. The highly capable Devine had never been entirely comfortable in New York, and when the opportunity came to return to the club where he had spent so many years, he took it. Devine's replacement was Johnny Murphy, a Mets front-office fixture since the team's inception. Murphy was another embodiment of the old New York tie, having been an ace relief pitcher for the great Yankee teams of the 1930s.

Nobody could have anticipated it, of course, but the 1968 New York Mets were a team gearing up to make history in the universe of baseball. Averaging twenty-six years of age, they were the youngest Mets club ever, and significantly many of the key players were home-grown products. Granted, there were no batting champions, no home-run sluggers (the team batted just .228), but the team was playing with a livelier spirit and deeper sense of pride than had any previous Mets outfit. Much of this derived from maturing players and from the rare chemistry that was evolving among them, and much of it came from the strong, quiet skills and patience of Gil Hodges.

Many of the miracle workers of the following year were in place now: Kranepool, Boswell, Harrelson, and the veteran Charles (at thirty-three the team's oldest player) comprised the infield. Jerry Grote was the catcher. The outfield was Swoboda, Jones, and a key addition, Tommie Agee.

Agee had been American League Rookie of the Year with the White Sox in 1966, batting .273 with 22 home runs and 44 stolen bases. In 1967, he had slumped badly in all departments and the White Sox became disenchanted and put him on the trading block. Hodges, who had watched Agee for two years and admired his hustling, nononsense style of play, urged the club to go after him. On December 15, 1967, the Mets sent their top hitter Tommy Davis, pitchers Jack Fisher and Billy Wynne, and a minor leaguer to Chicago for Agee and Al Weis, a light-hitting utility infielder. In an earlier deal, the Mets had sent infielder Bob Johnson to the Reds for power-hitting outfielder Art Shamsky. The mosaic's final pieces were now being inserted.

But what made optimism about the club genuine was its pitching. It was a staff filled with strong young arms, a staff suddenly the equal of almost any in the league. Seaver had posted a 16–12 season, with five shutouts, 205 strikeouts, and an ERA of 2.20. Jerry Koosman set a club record for victories with a 19–12 record and tied a league record for shutouts by a rookie with seven (last achieved by Grover Cleveland Alexander in 1911). His 2.08 ERA was the lowest in Mets history.

Along with Seaver and Koosman, there was Nolan Ryan. Slowed by injuries and stints of military service, the young Texan was only 6–9, but fanned 133 in 134 innings, throwing a fastball so hard that, as one batter said, "I always expected to see his arm come flying after it." Behind their starters the Mets had bullpen strength in righties Cal Koonce and Ron Taylor. Overall, the staff's collective ERA of 2.72 was bettered by only three other teams.

If it was a ninth-place finish in 1968, then it was a strong one, with many positive aspects, chief among them the best team record ever—73–89. A losing season yes, but hardly an embarrassing one. Also, Hodges's club was interesting enough to kick the attendance up by more than 200,000 to nearly 1,800,000, second in the league only to the pennant-winning Cardinals.

Very early on—April 15, to be exact—the Mets treated their new skipper to one of their now patented bizarre games. In a 24-inning, 6-hour, 6-minute marathon, the Mets lost to Houston 1–0 in the Astrodome. The game's only run scored in the bottom of the 24th when shortstop Al Weis erred on what should have been an inning-ending double-play ball. In terms of innings, it was the longest night game in history; it was the longest game ever played to a conclusion, and it set a mark with its 23 consecutive scoreless innings. Improving though they might be, the Mets showed that they still retained their penchant for the unique.

As the Mets were winding down their season with high hopes for 1969, a sobering event took place. It was in Atlanta, on September 24. After complaining of chest pains before the game, Hodges was taken to a hospital. A mild heart attack was diagnosed. It was the opinion of the doctors that after a period of rest, Hodges would be able to resume his normal life-style. This is, of course, one of the general therapies prescribed for heart-attack victims. But in this case the victim was the manager of a big-league baseball team. Given the pressures, the day-to-day irregularities in sleeping and eating due to the obligations of incessant travel, there was some doubt in the minds of baseball people whether Hodges could, or should, return.

But there was never any doubt in the big man's mind. After four weeks in the hospital, Hodges emerged, determined to pick up where he had left off. With a strong medical go-ahead, he plunged back into the business of making the Mets a better team in 1969.

Among the thinking and planning the Mets had to do for 1969 was the preparation for a radical new structure in baseball. The National League had voted to expand again, taking in two new teams, Montreal and San Diego. In order to avoid the unwieldiness of a twelve-team league, it was decided to divide into two six-team divisions, Eastern and Western. The Eastern consisted of St. Louis, Pittsburgh, Philadelphia, Chicago, Montreal, and New York. The Western was made up of Los Angeles, San Francisco, Houston, Cincinnati, San Diego, and Atlanta.

Baseball was heading into the era of divisional play, and New York City was heading for the most stunning pennant race in its history.

Spring training 1966, with skipper Westrum eying the troops.

Left to right: Ken Boyer, Roy McMillan, Ron Hunt, and Ed Kranepool in St. Petersburg in 1966.

Left to right: Eddie Bressoud, Ken Boyer, Ed Kranepool in the spring of 1966. Bressoud shared the shortstop position with McMillan in 1966.

Ken Boyer (1966–67), one of the great third basemen in National League history, was obtained from the Cardinals for Charley Smith and Al Jackson. Though past his prime, Ken batted .266 with 14 homers in 1966.

Cleon Jones (1963–75). One of the fine outfielders in Mets history, Cleon's .340 batting average in 1969 is the highest ever by a Met.

Al Luplow (1966–67). Al, formerly an outfielder with the Cleveland Indians, batted .251 for the Mets in 1966.

Young catcher Jerry Grote getting some advice from the best possible source—Hall of Fame catcher Yogi Berra, then a coach with the Mets.

Churning up the Shea Stadium real estate is Ed Kranepool, safe at home. Reaching for the throw is Milwaukee catcher (and future Mets manager) Joe Torre. The action took place on April 17, 1966.

Darrell Sutherland (1964–66), a right-hander who turned in some good relief work for the Mets. In 1965 he had an ERA of 2.85.

Dick Selma (1965–68). There were few pitchers who could throw harder than this right-hander, but somehow he never made it big with the Mets. A 9–10 record in 1968 was his best.

First baseman Dick Stuart, a big basher in his day. The well-traveled Stuart was with the Mets briefly in 1966.

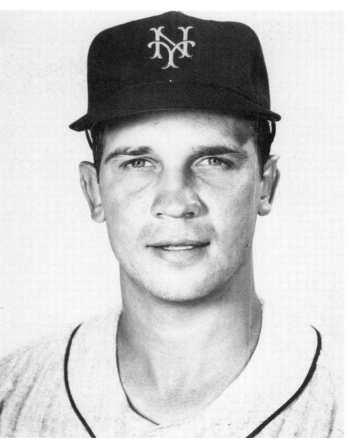

Dennis Ribant (1964–66). Dennis, a right-hander, had his best season in 1966 when he was 11–9.

This happened a lot to Mets outfielders in the early days. That's Jim Hickman *(left)* and Johnny Lewis trying to run down a long one shot out there by an opposing batter.

Jack Hamilton (1966–67). A hard-throwing right-hander, Jack worked the bullpen for the Mets, appearing in 57 games in 1966.

Tug McGraw.

Ralph Terry (1966–67). The one-time ace right-hander of the Yankees had a lame arm by the time he reached the Mets and wasn't able to contribute much.

Tommy Davis (1966). Tommy played just one year for the Mets, batted .302, then was traded to the White Sox in a deal for Tommie Agee.

Three Mets right-handers. *Left to right:* Jack Fisher, Bob Shaw, Don Cardwell. Shaw (1966–67) was 11–10 in 1966, while Cardwell (1967–70) proved a valuable spot starter for the club.

Second baseman Jerry Buchek (1967–68).

Utility infielder Bob Johnson (1967) made his one season with the Mets a productive one, batting .348 in 90 games. He was traded to Cincinnati for Art Shamsky.

Mets outfielders (left to right) Ron Swoboda, Tommy Davis, Don Bosch, and Cleon Jones. Bosch (1967–68) was supposed to fill the club's center field gap, but though a superb fielder, he was unable to hit big-league pitching.

THE NEW YORK METS

Gary Carter. © *1986 Ronald C. Modra*

Keith Hernandez.

Gary Carter. © *1986 Ronald C. Modra*

Howard Johnson.

Mookie Wilson.

Sid Fernandez.

Ray Knight.

Ron Darling.

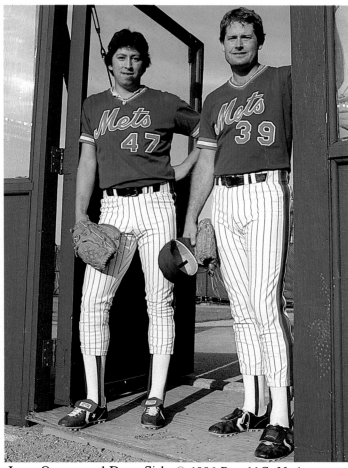

Jesse Orosco and Doug Sisk. © 1986 Ronald C. Modra

Wally Backman.

Tom Gorman.

Dwight Gooden. © 1986 Ronald C. Modra

Rusty Staub.

Rafael Santana.

Ed Lynch.

Danny Heep.

Howard Johnson.

George Foster.

Bruce Berenyi.

Rusty Staub.

George Foster.

Roger McDowell.

Keith Hernandez. © 1986 Ronald C. Modra

Darryl Strawberry.

Larry Stahl (1967–68), utility outfielder.

Jerry Grote (1966–77), considered by many the top defensive catcher of his time. His best year at the plate was .295 in 1975.

Ed Charles (1967–69). Ed gave the Mets a solid year at third base in 1968, batting .276 with 15 home runs.

An airborne Bud Harrelson trying for two.

They called Phil Linz "Supersub," and that's what the ex-Yankee was for the Mets in 1967–68.

Amos Otis, another one who got away. Amos played briefly for the Mets in 1967 and 1969, then was traded to Kansas City where he had a long and successful career.

Ken Boswell (1967–74). The Mets steady second baseman had his best year in 1969 when he batted .279. In the 1973 World Series he was 3-for-3 as a pinch-hitter.

Jerry Koosman (1967–78). The top left-hander in Mets history.

Gil Hodges, Mets manager (1968–71).

On deck, Bud Harrelson.

Letting one fly is Cal Koonce (1967–70). Used primarily in relief, Cal gave the Mets some excellent work.

Rookie Tom Seaver poses with Dodger veteran Don Drysdale in 1967.

Bing Devine *(left)*, and Johnny Murphy.

Tommie Agee (1968–72), the Mets' hard-playing center fielder. He led the world champions with 26 home runs in 1969.

Jerry Koosman.

Tom Seaver (1967–77, 1983).

MIRACLE

"MIRACLE MY EYE."

That was Tom Seaver's response to the most oft uttered description of 1969 and the New York Mets. "Miracle" implies some divine or supernatural intervention, and while the events of 1969 may have seemed just that to some people, Seaver had another, more pragmatic explanation: "What happened was that a lot of good young players suddenly jelled and matured all at once. The chemistry on that ball club was a beautiful thing to feel and to see in action. Everybody had to contribute because we weren't that powerful, and everybody did contribute."

The final moves had been made, the final ingredients added. Now it was shake well and go out and play. From the Atlanta organization the previous winter had come twenty-one-year-old third baseman Wayne Garrett, looking as though he might be the answer to that most troublesome position for the Mets. On June 15, the trading deadline, the Mets obtained a power-hitting first baseman to platoon with Kranepool—Donn Clendenon. The big man was ransomed from Montreal in exchange for infielder Kevin Collins and three minor-league pitchers. Already added to the pitching staff was right-hander Gary Gentry, whose slender physique belied the speed with which he could deliver a baseball to home plate.

The Las Vegas odds makers chalked the Mets in as 100–1 shots. "Some people," Seaver said, "thought even that was being charitable." The Mets players, however, knew better. For the first time in their history, a New York Mets club went into a season with a feeling of confidence. It was that pitching staff—Seaver, Koosman, Ryan, Gentry, McGraw, Cardwell, Taylor, Koonce—that made the opposition nervous. It was true the Mets did not have too much hitting, but with a staff that averaged around three earned runs a game, you didn't need too much hitting.

Nevertheless, the club got off to a poor start.

After 41 games they were 18–23, in fifth place, nine games behind Leo Durocher's league-leading Cubs. (A ninth-place finish in 1968, a slow start in 1969. If not fate, then at least it was a master scenarist that was at work here.) They had been 18–18, then lost five straight. It was at that point, on the night of May 28, that the Mets played the game that many of their players felt was a turning point. It was an 11-inning, 1–0 win over San Diego.

The Mets went on from there, sweeping three from the visiting Giants, then three more from the visiting Dodgers, the last game a 15-inning 1–0 tingler. So they headed west with a seven-game winning streak, a club record. The record soon expanded. In San Diego they swept the expansion Padres three straight, then won the opener in San Francisco for 11 straight before being stopped.

"I swear, it was electricity going through the team," Seaver recalled. "Everybody felt the same charge. We began getting stronger and stronger and feeling more and more confident. It went on from there, building."

The streak had lifted the club to second place, seven games behind Durocher's Cubs. Leo's club promised a hard summer, however. They had an array of long-ballers in Ernie Banks, Ron Santo, ex-Met Jim Hickman, Billy Williams, and Randy Hundley, plus a good double-play combination in Don Kessinger and Glenn Beckert. They also had three solid starters in righties Ferguson Jenkins and Bill Hands (20-game winners that year) and lefty Ken Holtzman.

In early July the Mets played the Cubs for the first "crucial" series in their eight-year history. Trailing Chicago by five games when the Cubs came into Shea for a three-game series, the Mets pulled to within three by taking the first two games. The second game featured a masterful performance by Seaver. In shutting down the Cubs 4–0, Seaver pitched 8⅓ perfect innings, losing his perfecto and his no-hitter when Jimmy Qualls singled in the ninth. The Cubs took the final game and left town four games up.

The following week the Mets went to Chicago and again took two of three and left town 3½ games behind. The Mets newfound mystique was never more evident than in this series. Utility infielder Al Weis, who hit only two home runs all season, stroked them both in this series, helping the club to its wins.

After that, it seemed that the Mets' dash for a pennant might become memory. The club floundered for the next few weeks, playing under .500 ball. On August 15 they were in third place, 9½ behind the Cubs and one behind the second-place Cardinals.

But then they suddenly surged again, winning nine of ten and charging to within five of the top. And kept charging. They took two from the Cubs at Shea in early September and a few days later, on September 10, they made a baseball equivalent of Sir Edmund Hillary's conquest of Everest by getting into first place when they beat Montreal while the Cubs were losing.

Slowly, steadily, the Mets went ahead, cementing their grip on the top rung. On September 12, Koosman and Cardwell pitched memorable 1–0 victories over the Pirates in a doubleheader, with the pitchers knocking in the run in each game.

On September 15, in St. Louis, the Mets scored one of the most improbable victories in their history. For many, it was the most telltale Mets win of the 1969 season. They beat Steve Carlton 4–3 on a pair of two-run homers by Swoboda—despite Carlton's major-league record 19 strikeouts. If it hadn't been before, then it was clearly evident now that nothing was going to stop these Mets.

The inevitable was fulfilled on September 24. On that night at Shea, before nearly 55,000 roaring customers, Gentry shut out the Cardinals 6–0, giving the Mets the Eastern Division title.

With the club winning 38 of its last 49 games, the Mets finished with a record of 100–62, a 27-game improvement over the previous year. The summer-long excitement was reflected at the turnstiles, with the Mets clearing the two-million barrier for the first time, drawing over 2,175,000 fans, and all of them satisfied.

Tom Seaver had emerged as a club leader and, not so incidentally, as baseball's best pitcher. The personable and charismatic fireballer racked up a 25–7 record, 208 strikeouts, and a 2.21 ERA (good enough for a Cy Young Award). Right behind him was Koosman with a 17–9 record and 2.28 ERA. Gentry was 13–12, while McGraw and Taylor were superb all year long out of the pen. Injuries and military commitments held Ryan to a 6–3 record, but when he was in there he was almost unhittable, with 92 strikeouts in 89 innings.

The hitting had been timely all season, and it had to be, because timely hitting was pretty much all they had. Jones was the top man with a .340 average (through the 1985 season still the highest in club history). Boswell was next with .279, followed by Agee with a hard .271 that included 26 home runs and 76 runs batted in. Agee's RBI total was tops on the club, an intriguing figure when one considers there were twenty-four other National League players who drove in more than the Mets' top man, including six on the Cincinnati Reds, who finished third in the West.

Grote, establishing himself as perhaps the game's premier defensive catcher, batted .252. ("If I was on the same team with him," said Johnny Bench, "I'd have to play third base.") Kranepool hit just .238, while his platoon partner Clendenon was at .252 with 12 homers. Another platoon player, Art Shamsky, gave the club a solid year's work, batting .300, with 14 home runs. Harrelson batted .248, Garret .218, and Weis .215.

Facing the Mets for the National League pennant in the first league championship series ever were the Atlanta Braves. The Braves couldn't match the Mets' pitching, but they had some genuine sock in the lineup with Orlando Cepeda, Felipe Alou, Rico Carty, and the great Henry Aaron.

What happened in that series evinced further proof that the Mets had turned the world upside down. When the starting pitching, uncharacteristically, faltered, the club put on, also uncharacteristically, a sustained three-game hitting attack.

With Seaver pitching a ragged game and trailing 5–4 in the top of the eighth of the opener in Atlanta, the Mets looped and rolled a series of hits, scored five runs, and went on to a 9–5 win, nailed down by Taylor.

The next day, with Koosman on the mound, the Mets came out like wildcats, scoring in each of the first five innings and building a 9–1 lead. But then Koosman came apart in the bottom of the fifth, the Braves scoring five to make it 9–6. Taylor and McGraw came in to hold it in place, Jones bombed a homer, and it was an 11–6 wrap.

The series moved to Shea the next day. Aaron put the Braves up 2–0 in the first with a long home run off Gentry. When the Braves threatened in the third inning, Hodges brought in Ryan, with Braves on second and third and none out. Young Nolan did his thing, fanning two and getting out of it.

The Mets scored one in the bottom of the third, and then in the fourth Boswell—three homers all season—put one out with a man on and the home team led 3–2. Ryan gave up a two-run shot to Cepeda in the top of the fifth and it was Atlanta 4–3. But the Mets came roaring back in the home half. Ryan singled and Wayne Garrett—one home run all season—lined one into the right-field bullpen, making it 5–4, Mets. Ryan made no further mistakes. The final was 7–4.

The Mets, the team of Marvelous Marv and Choo Choo and Hot Rod and Roadblock, the once-upon-a-time Amazin's of Casey, were National League champions, headed for the World Series. Their opponents? A team considered one of the greatest of all time, winners of 109 American League games: Earl Weaver's Baltimore Orioles.

It was a pair of supremely confident teams that joined for the 1969 World Series, the Orioles because they were used to winning, the Mets because they didn't believe they could lose. The same, but with a subtle difference.

Weaver's club had pitching to match the Mets': 20-game winning southpaws Dave McNally and Mike Cuellar, plus Jim Palmer and a deep bullpen consisting of Dick Hall, Eddie Watt, and lefty Pete Richert. Their combined 2.83 ERA was baseball's best.

The Baltimore regulars were all-star caliber at virtually every position, boasting both hitting and defense. In the cases of third baseman Brooks Robinson, shortstop Mark Belanger, and center fielder Paul Blair, the defense was a match for any in the game's history. At first base Weaver had Boog Powell (37 home runs), at second (make note of the name) Davey Johnson, and along with Blair in the outfield the great Frank Robinson and Don Buford. Behind the plate Weaver platooned Elrod Hendricks and Andy Etchebarren.

The Series opened on a bright Saturday afternoon in Baltimore. With a bang. Don Buford ripped Seaver's first pitch over the wall in right for a home run. Seaver was roughed up for three more runs in the fourth, the Mets managed one in the seventh, and Cuellar eased to a 4–1 win.

But a strange thing happened. In defeat the upstarts were buoyed rather than dejected. "I swear," Seaver said, "but we came into the clubhouse more confident than when we had left it. Somebody—I think it was Clendenon—yelled out, 'Dammit, we can beat these guys!' And we believed it. A team knows if they've been badly beaten or outplayed. And we felt we hadn't been. The feeling wasn't that we had lost, but *Hey, we nearly won that game*. We hadn't been more than a hit or two from turning it around. It hit us like a ton of bricks. I tell you, that was the chemistry we had on the 'sixty-nine Mets, these sudden surges of everybody thinking alike."

Thinking, and then doing. Koosman started game 2 against McNally and was brilliant. Given a one-run lead on a Clendenon homer in the top of the fourth, Jerry took a no-hitter into the bottom of the seventh. Then a single, stolen base, and single tied it. Then, with two out in the top of the ninth, singles by Charles, Grote, and Weis made it 2–1, Mets. The Orioles threatened in the bottom of the ninth, but Ron Taylor came in to get the last out. The Series was even.

As Buford had opened things up in Baltimore with a home run, so did Agee in New York, taking a Palmer pitch out of the park. Gentry worked steadily while his mates came pecking at Palmer for two more in the second (actually it was Gentry who sent them in with a double). It was in the top of that inning that Agee made the first of two heroic catches. With two Orioles on base, he made a spectacular, running, one-hand grab of a shot by Hendricks that saved two runs.

In the top of the seventh Gentry suddenly walked three in a row with two out. In came Ryan to face Blair. Paul tagged one into the right-center alley, and Agee, running long and hard, slid on one knee and grabbed the ball just before it struck the grass. Three more runs saved. The final was 5–0 (with five for Agee in the "saved" column).

Up two games to one now, the Mets gave the Orioles a dose of the magic that had so bemused the National League all summer. With Seaver nursing a 1–0 lead (set up by Clendenon's second-inning homer off Cuellar), the Orioles tied it with one in the ninth and might have had more except for another diving outfield grab, this time by Swoboda.

In the bottom of the 10th, fate put its shoulder to the Mets' wheel. Grote opened with a gift double that Blair lost in the sun. Rod Gaspar came in to run for Grote. Harrelson, the next batter, was walked intentionally. J. C. Martin came up to bat for Seaver. The Orioles countered with lefty Pete Richert. Martin, as expected, bunted. Richert fielded it and fired to first, but his throw hit Martin on the wrist. The ball bounded into short right field and Gaspar scored.

Photographs later showed that Martin had been running in fair territory when struck by the peg, but it was too late then. Mets magic had reached the point where it was now clouding an umpire's judgment.

Needing just one more to make America's moon landing a few months before seem like a mundane achievement, Hodges sent Koosman out to face McNally. Despite an early 3–0 Baltimore lead, inevitability hung over Shea Stadium—crepe for the Orioles, poised rockets for the Mets.

In the bottom of the sixth, Jones was awarded first base after being hit on the foot by a McNally pitch—or he was after Hodges showed the ball to Umpire Lou DiMuro with a smudge of shoe polish on it. Clendenon followed with his third homer of the Series and now the Mets were down by one. Then in the bottom of the seventh, Al Weis, perhaps the lightest stick on the club, hit a game-tying homer. In the bottom of the eighth, Jones doubled, Swoboda doubled him in and later scored on a grounder for a 5–3 Mets lead.

With one on and two out in the top of the ninth, Koosman induced Davey Johnson to fly to Jones in left. Cleon caught it, made his now-famous drop to one knee for a moment, and then raced in—to join his mates in celebration and to escape the tens of thousands of boisterous well-wishers and celebrants who were pouring out of the stands to share in the excitement as they had after the division clinching against the Cardinals and the pennant winner against the Braves.

In eight years the Mets had risen from a gleam in the eye of William Shea and his determined associates and hoisted themselves to the pinnacle of their profession. Twenty-five talented, spirited, and magnificently cohered young athletes had become instant, and lasting, legend.

Another big turnout at Shea.

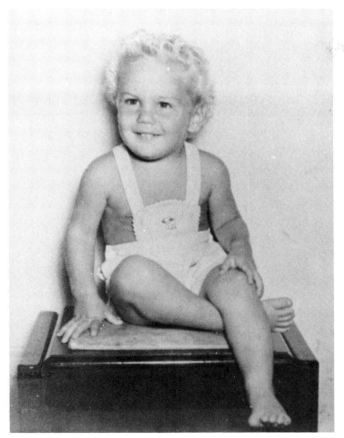

Tom Seaver, somewhere between infancy and the Hall of Fame.

Jerry Koosman.

Donn Clendenon (1969–71). The big first baseman brought some needed sock to the club. In 1970 he hit 22 homers and drove in 97 runs.

Wayne Garrett (1969–76), one of the better third base-men in Mets history. His best was .266 in 1975.

Jerry Grote.

Ron Swoboda (1965–70). One of the Mets' most popular players, "Rocky" had a top of .281 in 1967. He hit 19 homers in his rookie year.

Ron Taylor (1967–71). One of the mainstays of the Mets bullpen, Ron was particularly effective in the 1969 championship year with a 9–4 record and 2.72 ERA.

Standing for the National Anthem, *left to right:* Duffy Dyer, Ed Kranepool, Gil Hodges, Ken Boswell.

You're looking right down the barrel of the Nolan Ryan shotgun.

Tommie Agee sliding home. Making the play for the Cardinals is Tim McCarver, future New York Mets television announcer.

Gary Gentry (1969–72). The Mets fastballer had his top year in 1969 when he was 13–12.

An intense Gil Hodges follows the action.

It's the top of the eighth inning (see scoreboard) and Tom Seaver is working on a perfect game. A ninth-inning single cost him his no-hitter and perfect game.

Bud Harrelson. Coach Eddie Yost is next to him.

Ed Kranepool. His best year was 1975 when he batted .323. In 1974 he was 17-for-35 as a pinch-hitter.

Utility infielder Al Weis (1968–71). A sparkling glove man, but a .219 lifetime hitter, he surprised everyone with a .455 batting average against the Orioles in the 1969 World Series.

Tug McGraw.

Cal Koonce.

Tug McGraw letting one rip.

Jerry Koosman. In 1969 he had 17 wins, 6 shutouts, and a
2.28 ERA. You'd be laughing too.

Cleon Jones checking the fan mail.

Tommie Agee (*left*) and Gary Gentry.

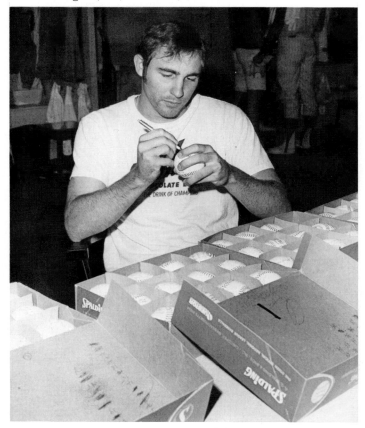

Ken Boswell attending to a big-league chore.

Don Cardwell pitching BP in Florida.

How young, how gifted. *Left to right:* Tom Seaver, Nolan Ryan, Jerry Koosman.

Art Shamsky (1968–71). Art's best was .300 and 14 home runs in 1969.

Rod Gaspar (1969–70), utility outfielder.

Jim Gosger (1969, 1973–74), utility outfielder.

Duffy Dyer (1968–74). A strong second-string catcher, Duffy would have been the regular on a lot of clubs.

J. C. Martin (1968–69). The veteran catcher was a capable backup for Jerry Grote.

Jim McAndrew (1968–73). Jim pitched some very good ball for the Mets, with an 11–8 record in 1972 his best year.

Jack DiLauro (1969). A southpaw, Jack pitched sparingly but effectively for the world champions.

Tom Seaver.

One of the fine keystone combinations in Mets history— Bud Harrelson (left) and Ken Boswell.

Gary Gentry and the Mets have just shut out the Cardinals on September 24, 1969, to clinch the Eastern Division title, much to the delight of their fans.

Another memorable moment from the 1969 World Series: J. C. Martin is about to be hit on the wrist by the peg from pitcher Pete Richert (no. 24) and the ball will carom away and allow the winning run to score. The photo clearly shows Martin running in fair territory, for which the Orioles contended he should have been declared out. In the foreground are *(left to right):* Boog Powell, Elrod Hendricks, and Richert; in the rear *(left to right):* Umpire Larry Napp, Dave Johnson, Martin, and coach Yogi Berra.

That ball going over the fence was the first Mets pitch thrown in the 1969 World Series. Tom Seaver threw it, Baltimore's Don Buford hit it, and Ron Swoboda made a game but futile effort to catch it.

Ron Swoboda diving to make his famous catch of a Brooks Robinson line drive in the ninth inning of game 4.

Tommie Agee making his memorable backhand grab of Elrod Hendrick's line drive with two on and two out in the top of the fourth inning of game 3 of the 1969 World Series. The action took place at Shea.

The joyous spontaneity of winners. Jerry Koosman leaping into the arms of Jerry Grote seconds after the Mets became world champs.

A champagne-splattered Gil Hodges accepting congratulations in the Mets clubhouse after the triumph over Weaver's Orioles.

Donald Grant (center) about to be baptized by some brew after the World Series victory. The man about to douse the boss is Tug McGraw. Jerry Grote seems to think beer is for drinking.

A veritable human explosion engulfs Shea minutes after the end of the 1969 Series.

Gil and Mrs. Hodges lead the victory parade down Fifth Avenue.

Jerry Koosman.

AFTER THE MIRACLE

IT IS A CERTAINTY IN BASEBALL THAT there will be a world champion every year. Play out your season and there will be division winners, your league championship series and there will be pennant winners, your World Series and there will be, finally, a champion. Play long enough and somebody has to win it. Looking back at 1969, however, it seems that the Mets, as with no other team before or since, were *destined* to win it. From Tom Seaver's golden arm to J.C. Martin's fortuitously placed wrist, from Tommie Agee's scintillating catches to Cleon Jones's shoe polish, even the most logical person would have to think, at least occasionally, that it all seemed to have been written in some celestial ledger eons ago.

You can't top a world championship; you can only hope to equal it and thus regenerate and re-create the joy and excitement. But there was no way the Mets could, even by repeating, equal what they had wrought in 1969. The '69 Mets had already been mythologized and lofted to some unreachable realm.

So 1970 was going to be anticlimactic no matter what happened (except at the box office, where the Mets outdid themselves with nearly 2,700,000 paid admissions).

The 1970 club did not look all that different from the 1969 club. Still trying to shore up third base, the Mets in December traded for Kansas City's Joe Foy. Not only did Foy fail to do the job, but the man the club traded for him was Amos Otis, a player of surpassing talents who went on to star for the Royals for many years. The Mets also added outfielder Dave Marshall and lefty Ray Sadecki, obtaining them from the Giants in exchange for infielder Bob Heise and outfielder Jim Gosgar.

Early in the new year, on January 14, General Manager Johnny Murphy died of a heart attack. Five days later he was replaced by the club's di-

rector of player personnel, Bob Scheffing, a former big-league catcher and manager.

The 1970 Mets stayed in the race until the final weeks, then slipped and finished third with an 83–79 record. A few years before, that record would have caused exultation, but now it was considered an "off year."

The top hitter in 1970 was Clendenon with a .288 batting average, 22 home runs, and 97 runs batted in. Agee was next with .286 and 24 homers, and then came Jones, who fell off from .340 to .277. Overall, the club hit better than they did in 1969; it was on the mound where they slipped. Seaver was 18–12, though he did lead the league with 283 strikeouts and 2.81 ERA. Arm miseries in the first half of the season held Koosman to a 12–7 record. Gentry fell to 9–9, while right-hander Jim McAndrew, counted on as the fourth starter, was only 10–14. Nolan Ryan was 7–11, despite his extraordinary stuff. Neither Taylor nor McGraw matched their 1969 work, though the pen was strengthened by right-hander Danny Frisella, who gave the club some good work.

The most overwhelming individual performance of the year was turned in by Seaver on April 22, against San Diego. The Mets ace had a Shea crowd roaring with delight as he tied a record with 19 strikeouts and established another by fanning the last ten in a row. Seaver, Ryan, and Gentry created some early excitement by pitching one-hitters in the opening weeks of the season, while from April 29 to September 27 Ken Boswell set a record by playing 85 straight games at second base without an error. These were positive accomplishments, duly noted. But there weren't enough.

Finishing third, the Mets were a game behind second-place Chicago and six behind a hard-hitting Pittsburgh club. These Pirates, with the heavy lumber of Roberto Clemente, Willie Stargell, Manny Sanguillen, Al Oliver, Richie Hebner, Dave Cash, and others, were set to dominate the division for the next half dozen years.

Soon after the close of the 1970 season, the Mets, unhappy with Foy, went back into the third-base market. The man they got this time was Bob Aspromonte. Bob was a thirty-two-year-old who had played part time for Atlanta in 1970 and batted .213.

The following spring, before the start of the 1971 season, the club made a trade that dismayed many of their followers when they sent Ron Swoboda to Montreal in exchange for a young center fielder of great defensive repute named Don Hahn. Giving up Swoboda, a colorful, sometimes unpredictable performer with a gift for the dramatic, who had become something of a Shea Stadium folk hero, was explainable on two counts. For one thing, "Rocky" had been with the club for six years and was evidently not going to fulfill his early promise. In those six years he had lifted his batting average out of the .240's just once. The other reason was this: Agee was having more and more trouble with his knees and the Mets wanted a dependable glove to back him up, just in case.

The only differences in the starting lineup in 1971 were Aspromonte at third and farm product Ken Singleton in the outfield. The twenty-four-year-old Singleton was a big, strong switch-hitter, and the Mets had high hopes for him.

The 1971 season was highly disappointing for the Mets. Hodges's boys finished tied for third with Durocher's Cubs, 14 games behind Pittsburgh. Adding to front-office discomfort was a 400,000 drop in attendance, although they still finished over the two-million mark. The mystique of the Mets had been predicated on two wildly opposing extremes—Stengel's lovable losers and Hodges's astonishing winners. There was a danger now of the Mets settling in as just another competent, no longer unique ball club.

But whatever else the Mets had or didn't have, there was Tom Seaver, growing year by year into one of baseball's truly great pitchers. In 1971 he was 20–10, again leading in strikeouts with 289 and ERA with a parsimonious 1.76. But behind Seaver there was some spottiness. Gentry, at 12–11, seemed molded as a .500 pitcher. Injuries dropped Koosman to 6–11, while wildness made a 10–14 pitcher of Ryan. McGraw and Frisella were strong coming out of the bullpen, but there just weren't enough games to save.

The hitting again was modest, with Jones leading the club with a .319 mark. Behind him was Agee at .285, Kranepool .280, Boswell .273, Grote .270, and so on down the lineup. Both Aspromonte (.255) and Singleton (.245) were disappointments.

Some more of the magic names of 1969 began disappearing after the close of the 1971 season. Al Weis had been dropped during the summer, and later Art Shamsky and Ron Taylor were traded and Donn Clendenon released. Also released was Aspromonte, whose failure to hit led directly to the most infamous trade in Mets history.

Continuing to be frustratd by their inability to find a regular third baseman, the Mets decided to plunge deep into the marketplace and once and for all solve the problem. The man they coveted was California's veteran shortstop Jim Fregosi (he had never played an inning at third in his big-league career). Fregosi had been a premier player in the American League for years, but in 1971 he had the worst season of his career, suffering injuries and batting .232. Nevertheless, this was the man the Mets wanted. To get him they parted with Nolan Ryan and three minor leaguers.

Why did the Mets trade the man destined to become the most prolific strikeout pitcher in baseball history, one whom they admitted had an arm of limitless potential? Several reasons. They had simply made up their minds that the twenty-four-year-old pitcher was never going to harness the power in his explosive fastball. (In 1971 Ryan continued to walk batters with almost the same frequency with which he fanned them.) Another reason was the Mets, with Seaver, Koosman, Gentry, and highly regarded rookie southpaw Jon Matlack, were pitcher rich.

On April 2, 1972, Hodges and his coaches, Rube Walker, Joe Pignatano, and Eddie Yost, were in West Palm Beach, Florida. As they were returning to their motel after a round of golf, Walker said, "What time do you want to go to dinner, Gil?"

The question was never answered. Without a sound, Hodges suddenly pitched backward and with tree-trunk rigidity fell, his head striking the stone sidewalk with a sickening knock. The skipper of the New York Mets was dead, victim of a brutally sudden and fatal heart attack, two days short of his forty-eighth birthday.

Throughout baseball there was genuine sadness and mourning for Gil Hodges. He had spent nearly three decades on the big-league scene, as slugging first baseman and successful manager; he had been a man of high character, God-fearing, devoted to his family. And an intriguing man, for there had always seemed to be something at the core of this immensely strong, soft-spoken, and slyly witty man that had never quite been penetrated by those who felt they knew him.

For the Mets it was a time of terrible ambivalence. The grief for their loss was sincere and ran deep, but a new season was approaching and they needed a manager.

On April 6, the Mets announced the name of their new skipper. It was a surprise to no one—Lawrence Peter ("Yogi") Berra, former catcher and pennant-winning manager for the Yankees, one of baseball's best-known and well-liked personalities; one of the game's few names, in fact, that transcended it and was known to the non-baseball world. The Berra legend was already a quarter of a century in the making, and it came with a full complement of malaprops and apocryphal stories. But those who knew him, knew that much of the Yogi Berra legend was the product of newspapermen, and that Berra, in his milieu, was a very keen student of the profession he had been practicing with remarkable success for so many years. While he did mangle a phrase now and then, with Yogi it was important that you listen to what he was saying, not how; and what he said generally made very good sense.

The announcement of Berra's appointment was accompanied by another; the Mets had traded outfielder Ken Singleton, infielder Tim Foli, and first basemen–outfielder Mike Jorgenson to Montreal for hard-hitting outfielder Rusty Staub. That these announcements were made on the day of Hodges's funeral gives one a telling glimpse into the boardroom side of baseball, the cold-blooded practical side that must at all times keep the machinery geared and running. Grief, mourning, sentiment, it was all there, but it could not be allowed to impinge on reality's ongoing tide. Yogi Berra was manager and twenty-eight-year-old Rusty Staub was in the outfield. In Staub the Mets had a bona fide smacker, a .311-hitting, 97-RBI man the year before with Montreal. Also joining the club this year was John Milner, a left-handed, power-hitting first baseman–outfielder.

On May 11, the Mets added another "new" face to the team. In a move seasoned with sentiment more than anything else, they acquired Willie Mays from the Giants for pitcher Charlie Williams and cash.

The acquisition of Mays had been a longtime dream of that old New York Giants fan, Mrs. Joan Payson. With Willie no longer pulling the weight of his large contract, Giants owner Horace Stoneham made him available, and Mrs. Payson could not resist.

He was, of course, no longer the fabled Willie Mays, the greatest player since DiMaggio, and, some said, maybe the greatest ever. He was forty-one years old, slowed down considerably in the field and at the plate, no longer possessing that cannon of an arm. He was, in truth, something of a liability now in center and it was more prudent to play him at first base. Actually, outside of still being something of a drawing card, there was no place for Mays on the club. But there he was.

The club got off to a sizzling start in 1972, playing better than .700 ball in early June. But soon after, a series of disabling injuries to Staub, Harrelson, Grote, and Jones brought the team up short and dropped them into their third consecutive third-place finish, 13½ behind Pittsburgh.

It had been a highly disappointing year. Fregosi, with a broken thumb in spring training, never got untracked and continued the third-base jinx with a .232 batting average. Boswell hit just .211 and the club was ready to give up on him. Milner flashed some power with 17 homers but batted only .238. Agee, unhappy at being displaced in center by Mays now and then, batted .227, and the club already had his ticket punched. Staub, limited to just 66 games because of a broken hand, hit .293 and was sorely missed. Mays batted a respectable .267, but his fielding deficiencies were now glaring.

Seaver was 21–12, McAndrew 11–8, Koosman 11–12, while Rookie of the Year Matlack was 15–10. Gentry slumped to 7–10, leaving his employers disenchanted. McGraw continued as the bullpen ace, with 8 wins and 27 saves.

On September 30, Matlack made the trivia lists when he served up a two-base hit to Pittsburgh's Roberto Clemente. It was the Pirate great's 3,000th and last big-league hit. On New Year's

Eve, Clemente lost his life when the plane on which he was taking food and medical supplies to earthquake-smashed Managua, Nicaragua, crashed into the ocean soon after taking off from San Juan, Puerto Rico.

With another frustrating season behind them, the Mets began preparing for 1973. The likable Yogi would be back as manager. Back also, to the unspoken dismay of certain of his teammates, would be Mays. But some other familiar names would not. On November 1, the Mets swapped pitchers Gary Gentry and Danny Frisella to Atlanta for second baseman Felix Millan and southpaw George Stone. Four weeks later, on November 27, another of the glory boys of '69, Tommie Agee, was sent to Houston for outfielder Rich Chiles and pitcher Buddy Harris—essentially, a giveaway of Agee. The housecleaning continued on December 1 with the swap of outfielder Dave Marshall to San Diego for Pitcher Al Severinsen, who never pitched for the Mets.

None of these moves seemed particularly dramatic, although in time, the acquisition of Millan would prove to be a key in the transformation of the club. The team looked as though it were entering a period of stagnation, locked into third place, with the chances of dropping apparently much better than those of rising.

The Mets, however, had a few things going for them as they headed for the 1973 season: those three fine starters, Seaver, Koosman, and Matlack, a torrid McGraw in the bullpen, and the peculiarities of divisional play.

Tom Seaver.

Left to right: Joe Foy, Dave Marshall, and Ray Sadecki. Foy (1970), obtained from Kansas City for Amos Otis, was supposed to be the answer to the third-base problem. He lasted just one year. Marshall (1970–72) was a left-handed-hitting utility outfielder. Sadecki (1970–74, 1977) gave the Mets some good left-handed pitching, starting and relieving.

Nolan Ryan loosening up the golden arm in spring training, 1970.

Tommie Agee (*left*) and Jerry Koosman.

Tom Seaver (*left*) and Dean Chance. The Mets obtained Chance, a former Cy Young Award winner in the American League, to help in the 1970 pennant drive, but the one-time ace had little left.

Ron Swoboda.

Ray Sadecki.

Jim McAndrew.

The heart of the Mets bullpen in 1970. *Left to right:* Tug McGraw, Danny Frisella, and Ron Taylor. Frisella (1967–72) gave the Mets top work coming out of the pen. In 1977, at the age of thirty, Danny lost his life in a motor vehicle accident in Arizona.

Bob Aspromonte. Bob was 1971's third-base candidate, but he batted .225 and lasted just the one year.

Jerry Grote.

Teddy Martinez (1970–74) had a smooth glove that was at home in both the infield and outfield. He batted .288 as a part-timer in 1971.

Jim Fregosi (1973–74). It wasn't his fault, but the Mets traded Nolan Ryan to get Fregosi. The 1972 answer to the third-base problem, Jim batted .232 and was gone the next year.

Tim Foli (1970–71, 1978–79). "Scrappy" was the word they used for this young shortstop.

Wayne Garrett.

Mike Jorgensen (1968–71, 1980–83). A valuable bench man, the versatile Jorgensen was a fine glove at both first base and in the outfield.

Don Hahn (1971–74), a light-hitting but smooth-fielding center fielder.

Gary Gentry giving it his all.

Yogi Berra, Mets manager (1972–75).

Ken Singleton (1970–71). The big, switch-hitting out-fielder was traded to Montreal with Foli and Jorgensen for Rusty Staub.

Ed Kranepool.

Buzz Capra (1971–73). Arm miseries curtailed the career of this promising young pitcher.

Bud Harrelson.

Rusty Staub (1972–75, 1981–85).

John Milner (1971–77). A first baseman-outfielder with some pop in his bat, John peaked with 23 homers in 1973.

Willie Mays.

Tommie Agee.

Cleon Jones.

Jon Matlack (1971–77). One of the finer pitchers in Mets history, Jon's best year was 1976 when he was 17–10. In 1974 and again in 1976, he led the league in shutouts.

Tug McGraw.

ANOTHER PENNANT

IT WASN'T AS STUNNING OR IMPROBAble as 1969, it didn't have—couldn't have—the drama or electricity or wondrous magic, but in their acquired tradition, the Mets' 1973 pennant victory was most unorthodox. For one thing, there were three clubs in the league that posted better won-lost records than the Mets in 1973, but they were all in the Western Division (Cincinnati, Los Angeles, and San Franciso). For another thing, every club but San Diego bettered the Mets' .246 club batting average, and every club but San Diego outscored them.

Nevertheless.

It was hardly an inspiring season for anyone in the National League East. No team seemed capable of taking charge. On July 26, the Mets were in last place, but only 7½ games behind. Nor was it to get better in a hurry. On August 16, they were 12 games below .500, with 44 left to play. It was shaping up as a most forgettable season.

At the end of August, the Mets were in last place, nine games under .500, but, in the balanced mediocrity of that year's Eastern Division, just 5½ out of first. The mathematical inequities of divisional play were beginning to show up. It became more and more ludicrous. On September 11, the Mets were in fourth place, five games under .500, but just three games out. Ahead of them were St. Louis, Pittsburgh, and Montreal. It was wide open.

With Tug McGraw urging his teammates on and celebrating victories with what soon became the catch phrase of 1973, "You gotta bee-lieve!" the Mets kept zigging and zagging away from would-be tacklers and, taking an occasional sideswipe, headed for this most unlikely of pennants. Down the stretch, Yogi, that imperturbable veteran of many a pennant race, ran four starters at the league: Seaver, Koosman, Matlack, and Stone, with the suddenly unhittable McGraw coming out of the pen with boisterous—and justi-

fied—confidence. (For his last 19 games, the screwball-throwing lefty showed 12 saves, 5 wins, and an ERA of 0.88.)

After sweeping a three-game series from the Pirates at Shea on September 21, the Mets' record stood at an even 77–77. But that .500 record was good enough for first place and a half-game lead. Illustrating just how dense the crowd was at the top, fifth-place Chicago was just 2½ out.

But the Mets did not falter. They finished with an 82–79 record and .509 winning percentage, lowest for any winner anywhere. The Cardinals were second, 1½ behind, Pittsburgh next at 2½, Montreal third at 3½, and Chicago fifth, 5 games out.

Heading into their second league championship series, the Mets found waiting for them Sparky Anderson's Cincinnati Reds. The Reds had won the West with a 99–63 record, 16½ games better than the Mets. Sparky's lineup included Pete Rose, Tony Perez, Joe Morgan, Johnny Bench, and rookies Dan Driessen and Ken Griffey. The pitching was headed by 19-game winner Jack Billingham, 18-game winning southpaw Don Gullett, and a solid bullpen headed by Pedro Borbon, Tom Hall, and Clay Carroll. Cincinnati was clearly the stronger team (except on the mound) and entered the best 3-of-5 series as favorites.

The opening game did nothing to dispel the Reds' aura of supremacy. Eighth- and ninth-inning home runs by Rose and Bench got them past Seaver, 2–1.

The following day, however, Staub's fourth-inning homer gave Matlack a 1–0 lead; the talented lefty defended it tenaciously all the way. A four-run Mets ninth made it a 5–0 two-hitter for Matlack.

The series now moved to Shea. The Mets made it easy for Koosman by scoring nine runs and Jerry coasted to a 9–2 win. This game was highlighted by a scuffle at second base between Rose and Harrelson that ensued after Pete bowled Harrelson over while trying to break up a double play. Harrelson reacted angrily and the two men tangled. The brief swing-out aroused the ire of Mets fans and made Rose a target for Shea Stadium wrath for years later.

The Reds, and Rose, showed their mettle the next day, winning 2–1 in 12 tension-wracked innings. The winning run? Pete's home run in the top of the 12th. The blow nullified a fine pitching effort by Stone and McGraw.

It came down to a fifth and deciding game, with Seaver going for the Mets, Billingham for the Reds. Seaver was not at his best, but some key hits by Kranepool, Garrett, Jones, and pinch-hitter Willie Mays gave the Mets a 7–2 lead going into the ninth. With Seaver faltering, and over 50,000 Mets fans frenzied and turning rowdy, McGraw, fittingly, came in and hosed down the Reds. The New York Mets were the unlikely 1973 National League pennant winners.

Yogi Berra had become only the second manager to win pennants in both leagues (the other was Joe McCarthy). And Yogi had done it despite a season's-long series of injuries to key players: Harrelson missed over 50 games, Jones 70 games, and Grote nearly half the season.

But Millan had played superbly at second base and batted .290, Staub hit a productive .279, and Garrett, after the midseason departure of Fregosi, .256 with 16 home runs. Seaver won 19, again took strikeout (251) and ERA (2.08) honors, while Koosman and Matlack each won 14, and George Stone contributed a crucial 12–3 record. McGraw, of course, had topped the relief pitchers.

Following the season's pattern, which had seen them win the division on the final day of the season, and the pennant in the final game of the league championship series, Yogi's heroes took the World Series to a wrenching seven games before finally losing to the Oakland A's, a club in the midst of a run of five consecutive division titles and three successive world championships.

Dick Williams's team was the team of Reggie Jackson, Joe Rudi, Bert Campaneris, Sal Bando, Gene Tenace, and three 20-game winners—Jim ("Catfish") Hunter, Ken Holtzman, and Vida Blue, backed up by the great relief pitcher Rollie Fingers.

The Series opened in Oakland. It was a duel between two top left-handers, Oakland's Holtzman and New York's Matlack. The A's won it, 2–1.

Game 2 was a long and untidy affair—12 innings that consumed 4 hours and 13 minutes. The Mets used five pitchers, the A's six, and the A's contributed five errors. The Mets were winning 6–4 in the bottom of the ninth, when the A's tied it. The Oakland rally got a boost when the aging Mays was unable to reach a fly ball that dropped for a double. It was the last time Willie Mays was to appear in the field in a major-league game. In the top of the 12th, however, Willie drove in the go-ahead run with a clutch two-out single in a four-run outburst. The New Yorkers won it, 10–7.

The Series then crossed the continent and set up business in New York. Game 3 was another extra-inning affair, which Oakland won in 11, 3–2. Seaver worked the first eight, giving up just two runs and fanning twelve.

Game 4 belonged to Jon Matlack and Rusty Staub. Matlack stopped the A's 6–1, giving up just three hits in the eight innings he worked. Staub popped a three-run homer in the bottom of the first and a two-run single in the bottom of the fourth, giving him five of the six RBIs.

The next day it was Koosman and McGraw combining on a three-hit, 2–0 shutout, with Cleon Jones doubling home a run in the second and Don Hahn tripling in the other in the sixth. The Mets were now just one game away from their second world championship.

The Series returned to Oakland. Game 6 saw a matchup of aces, Seaver versus Hunter. Tom was off in his game just a little; not much, but enough. Hunter and two relievers nudged the Mets aside by a 3–1 score.

The grand climax of the 1973 baseball season had Matlack starting against Holtzman. In the bottom of the fourth, Campaneris broke a scoreless tie with a two-run homer. Reggie followed with a second two-run shot in that inning. It was 4–0 Oakland and the shadows began to grow longer. The Mets were unable to mount any sort of sustained attack against Holtzman or the Oakland bullpen brigade and went quietly in a 5–2 loss.

The 1973 season, the year of the unlikely pennant, was over.

Yogi Berra.

Jim McAndrew.

Left to right: Matlack, Seaver, Koosman, the Big Three pitchers of the Mets' 1973 pennant drive.

Second baseman Felix Millan (1973–77). Probably the Mets' all-time second baseman, he hit .290 in the 1973 pennant year and in 1975 set a club record with 191 hits.

Wayne Garrett.

John Milner.

Rusty Staub.

Cleon Jones.

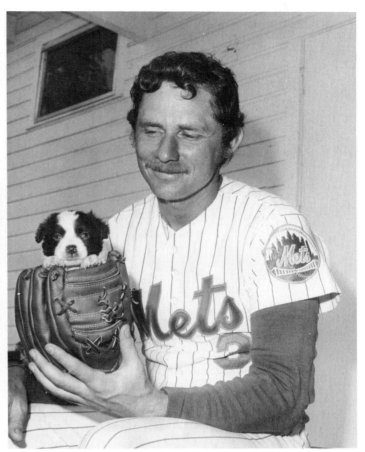

Bud Harrelson and friend. They say a good shortstop is supposed to pick up anything.

Jerry Grote.

Ken Boswell.

John Milner.

Willie Mays.

Jim Beauchamp (1972–73). A capable handyman, Jim got some key hits in the 1973 pennant drive.

Tug McGraw.

Ron Hodges (1973–84). An excellent backup catcher, Ron gave the Mets twelve years of good service.

George Theodore (1973–74). Although with the Mets for only two years, the colorful Theodore developed a devoted following. Nicknamed "The Stork," George played the outfield and a little first base.

Seaver and pitching coach Rube Walker. Rube worked for the Mets from 1968 through 1981, helping to develop the club's long line of fine young pitchers.

Jerry Koosman.

Jon Matlack.

Jon Matlack at work.

The long stride of Jerry Koosman.

Some heavy action in the 1973 World Series against Oakland. In the photo at the left, New York's Bud Harrelson is bounding into the plate as Oakland's Ray Fosse puts the tag on. In the photo at the right, Harrelson vaults away as on-deck batter Willie Mays stares at Fosse. The action occurred in the top of the 10th inning of game 2.

Following the action above, Umpire Augie Donatelli called Harrelson out, whereupon an irate Mays fell to his knees showing Augie by how much Harrelson was safe. It didn't help.

George Stone (1973–75), a talented left-hander, was 12–3 in 1973. Soon after, he suffered a rotator-cuff injury that effectively ended his career.

Harry Parker (1973–75). A right-hander, Harry was 8–4 in helping the Mets to the pennant in 1973.

Dave Kingman stepping into one.

THE QUIET YEARS

WITH THE MIRACLE PENNANT AND THE Unlikely Pennant now behind them, the Mets lapsed into what was to be a sort of aimless wandering for the next decade. Now and then there was a surge, now and then some sparkling individual performances; but generally, it was the quiet waters of fifth or sixth place. The winning touch was gone, and slowly the nostalgia, too, drained away as one after another, the gallants of the glory days moved on.

In 1974, Yogi brought the troops in fifth. Again the club was outhit by everyone in the league except San Diego and again outscored by everyone except San Diego. But now the lame attack was more telling, more glaring, because the pitching had leveled off. Bothered by a hip injury, Seaver was reduced to an 11–11 season, though when he needed 13 strikeouts in his final start for a record-setting 200 for a seventh consecutive season, the great right-hander went out and whiffed 14. Koosman was 15–11 and Matlack 13–15 (with seven shutouts), but the bullpen afforded little help as McGraw suffered through an atrocious year, nailing just three saves.

After the season, on October 13, new general manager Joe McDonald (he had replaced the retired Bob Scheffing) pulled a swap that would have some impact on the club's future. The Mets sent pitcher Ray Sadecki and a minor leaguer to the Cardinals for the veteran Joe Torre, a former MVP whose best days were behind him.

On December 3, the Mets subtracted another popular face when they dealt McGraw to the Phillies in a six-man deal that brought them, most notably, a young catcher named John Stearns who would gradually start filling in for and ultimately replace the injury-ridden Grote.

On February 28, 1975, the Mets scored a coup. For cash estimated at around $100,000, they acquired the Giants' explosive home-run hitter, Dave Kingman. A moody but undeniable talent,

Kingman had batted just .223 for San Francisco in 1974, striking out every third at-bat, but many of his 18 home runs had traveled breathtaking distances. Kingman, the Mets hoped, would provide the home-run power the club lacked, as well as generate some excitement.

The Mets were indeed stronger in 1975. Their .256 batting average was the highest in club history, and Kingman did supply some wallop with a team-record 36 home runs, while Staub's 105 RBIs made him the first Met to drive in 100. Again the club's greatest strength lay in its pitching, topped by Seaver's 22–9 record, good enough for a third Cy Young Award. Koosman was 14–13 and Matlack 16–12, but after that no one won more than seven. It all added up to an 82–80 season and a tie for third.

It also added up to the dismissal of Manager Berra, on August 6. His replacement for the rest of the season was coach Roy McMillan. Also gone, a week earlier, was Cleon Jones, released outright. The mythmakers of 1969 were rapidly thinning out.

As the season rolled to an end, there was a quick succession of news stories impinging on the Mets. On September 29, Casey Stengel died of cancer in California at the age of eighty-five. A few days later, on October 4, the club's popular "godmother" and principal owner, Mrs. Joan Payson, died at the age of seventy-two. If death delineates history, then the Mets' historical past was beginning to take shape, thirteen years after their origin.

In between the passing of these two nurturing spirits, the club on October 3 announced the hiring of their fifth full-time manager.

The new man was Joe Frazier. Frazier was the least known of Mets skippers, and the first without some connection with New York's baseball past. For the first time, the Mets were promoting from within, Frazier's elevation being the reward for leading into first place the team's top farm club, Tidewater in the International League. (His work at Tidewater in 1975 earned him the *Sporting News* accolade as Minor League Manager of the Year.)

Three days short of his fifty-third birthday when hired, Frazier had been a left-handed-hitting outfielder who had seen service briefly with Cleveland, St. Louis, Cincinnati, and Baltimore. Altogether, he had played in 217 games, leaving behind a modest legacy of ten home runs and a .241 lifetime batting average.

Two other announcements of note were forthcoming in the closing weeks of 1975. On December 6, Mrs. Lorinda de Roulet, daughter of the late Joan Payson, was named president of the Mets. (The critical decisions, of course, were still made by board chairman Donald Grant and G.M. Joe McDonald.)

On December 12, the Mets made what turned out to be a bad deal with Detroit. In exchange for veteran left-hander Mickey Lolich and outfielder Billy Baldwin, they sent the popular Rusty Staub and minor-league pitcher Bill Laxton. Lolich, once an outstanding pitcher, spent just one year with the Mets and then left, while Staub continued his sharp hitting for the Tigers.

The Mets started off well in 1976—on May 8 they were in first place with an 18–9 record; but then they plunged, losing 24 of their next 33, a prolonged nose dive that effectively took them out of the race. They ended in third place with an 86–76 record, the win total at that time being the second-best in their history. Still, they were 15 behind at the finish.

Koosman had his best year in 1976, winning 21 and losing 10, while Matlack was 17–10. Seaver, who had waged a holdout in spring training that grew increasingly acrimonious and left a strained relationship with Grant, was 14–11. Lolich, who the Mets had counted on as a strong fourth starter, was only 8–13.

Despite missing 40 games, Kingman still hit 37 home runs, but the fact that he drove in only 86 runs with that many homers indicates the bases were largely underpopulated much of the time.

After 1976, the club dropped into what, in retrospect, seems like a long dark age. From 1976 through 1983, their finishes read like this: sixth, sixth, sixth, fifth, fifth/fourth (in the strike-inter- rupted split season of 1981), sixth, sixth. The club's artistic decline brought with it a precipitous drop in attendance. From a peak of nearly 2,700,000 in 1970, they fell to under 800,000 in 1979.

For Mets fans, the ultimate blow to pride and loyalty came on June 15, 1977, for many still the most infamous date in club history. As culmination to the long bickering over money that had been going on between Seaver and Donald Grant, the club shocked and outraged its fans by trading the great star pitcher to the Reds.

From a public-relations perspective, the trade was a disaster. That the Mets were a failing team was apparent; that they still had one dominant asset was also apparent. But Seaver was for Mets fans more than a mound spectacular; he was a still highly effective symbol of past glory, and he instilled pride in the fans. Whatever else they might not have had, they still had as their very own the man generally acclaimed as baseball's premier pitcher. No matter how abrasive the relationship between Seaver and his employers had become, dealing him away was a serious miscalculation.

In return for the man who had become known, aptly, as "Tom Terrific," the Mets received some good ballplayers. The Reds sent them slick-fielding second baseman Doug Flynn, pitcher Pat Zachry, and outfielder Steve Henderson, each of whom gave the team some fine moments. Also in the deal was outfielder Dan Norman, who never quite made it in New York.

But there was more on that June 15. The Mets also traded their home-run-hitting threat Dave Kingman to San Diego for infielder Bobby Valentine and pitcher Paul Siebert. The rationale for this trade was that Kingman was probably going to become a free agent at the end of the season and the club would lose him anyway. But coming on top of the Seaver trade, aligned with the fact that the team got very little in return for their big buster, the Kingman trade only added to the growing disenchantment at Shea Stadium.

Earlier in the year, on May 31, the Mets had fired Manager Joe Frazier and replaced him with first baseman Joe Torre. Torre, who soon retired as a player, was the club's sixth manager and in certain respects his appointment reestablished the New York connection of Mets managers. Although he had spent most of his fine career with the Braves and Cardinals, Torre had grown up and played his first baseball in Brooklyn. When the thirty-six-year-old Torre retired as a player that June, he left behind a .297 lifetime batting average for his eighteen years in the major leagues, including an MVP season in 1971 when he led the league with a .363 batting average.

Torre was an able manager, with a veteran's incisive insights into the game and the ability to handle and motivate players. But it was the old story—a last-place team was a last-place team no matter how able the manager. The Mets did have some promising new players in outfielder Lee Mazzilli and catcher John Stearns, but there wasn't enough sock in the lineup. The once powerful pitching staff had also taken on a leaner look. Seaver was gone, and in 1977 Koosman was 8–20 and Matlack (who was traded that December) was 7–15.

Before what was to be a lackluster 1978 season opened, Harrelson and Millan were gone, Buddy traded to the Phillies and Felix sold all the way to Japan to play for the Taiyo Whales. After the season Koosman, who had suffered through a 3–15 record, was traded to the Minnesota Twins for two minor-league pitchers, one of whom was Jesse Orosco.

The biggest excitement to occur at Shea in 1978 occurred on the night of July 25. It was on this night that Pete Rose was trying to establish a new league record by hitting in 38 consecutive games. When Pete succeeded, he broke the old mark of 37 set by Tommy Holmes of the Boston Braves in 1945. Coincidentally, Holmes was a longtime Mets front-office employee, and when the new record was established, Tommy came out onto the field to congratulate Pete. (Rose went on to hit in 44 straight before being stopped in Atlanta.)

In 1979, the Mets dropped into last place on May 7 and never got out. Dropping with them was the attendance, down to an all-time low of 788,000. The Mets got some respectable hitting from Mazzilli (.303) and Steve Henderson (.306), but there was little pitching to speak of. Right-hander Criag Swan was the ace with a 14–13 record, but after him no pitcher won more than six games.

On November 19, 1979, it was announced that Mrs. de Roulet and her family had decided to sell its interest in the ball club. This was the beginning of the final phasing out of the club's original owners, and to many Mets fans it was long overdue. Under the guidance of Donald Grant and Mrs. de Roulet, the Mets had not kept step with baseball's changing structure, meaning primarily the advent of the free agent and reentry draft.

On January 24, 1980, ownership of the team changed hands. The group that bought the Mets, for an estimated $22 million (the largest amount ever paid for a ball club to that point), was headed by Nelson Doubleday and Fred Wilpon. Doubleday was head of the old and distinguished publishing company that bore his name, while Wilpon was a highly successful real-estate developer.

The new owners promised to spend money to get winning players and to make the club competitive. These were the standard promises of new ownership; but in this case they were genuinely meant and acted upon. Over the next few years, Doubleday, Wilpon, and their associates would demonstrate their eagerness to restore the New York Mets. But years it would take before the new partners were able to tear down their club and transmute it into that desired status of contender.

Hired as architect of this rebuilding was a consummate professional. He was Frank Cashen, who had spent ten years in the front office of the Baltimore Orioles (1966–75), helping that organization become the most successful in baseball. After leaving the Orioles, Cashen worked outside of baseball for three years before joining Commissioner Bowie Kuhn's office as administrator of baseball. It was from this job that the Mets wooed him and installed him as executive vice president and general manager.

Some of his impatient New York critics complained that Cashen lacked flair. Maybe. But it wasn't flair that built winning teams—it was patience, shrewd judgment, confidence in that judgment, and the courage to act upon it. All these Cashen possessed, and they were his style.

Refusing to be panicked into making moves that were merely player shuffling and public-relations balm, Cashen moved slowly. There certainly wasn't much encouragement in 1980—the team under Torre finished fifth, 24 games out of first place. Nevertheless, a highly significant move was made by the Mets on June 3. Last-place finishes had but one virtue: they assured a team an early pick in the June free-agent draft. In 1980, the Mets had first pick and they selected an eighteen-year-old outfielder from Los Angeles they deemed the nation's number-one amateur, a "do-it-all" power plant named Darryl Strawberry. Right then and there the Mets' future began turning brighter.

The 1980 season may have been another dismal serving—the Mets lost 38 of their last 49 games; but something must have been sparked at Shea, as the attendance jumped nearly 400,000 to almost 1,200,000.

Cashen remained on the side of caution. There were no wholesale shakeups after 1980. The most substantial move the team made—and a highly popular one it was—was to bring back Rusty Staub, signed out of the reentry draft. In February 1981, Cashen brought back another familiar face when he made a swap with the Cubs—Steve Henderson for Dave Kingman. Hoping to add still more hitting, Cashen in May made another move, though an unfortunate one, when he traded hard-throwing reliever Jeff Reardon to Montreal for outfielder Ellis Valentine. Valentine was a player of abundant talent, but he simply never made it with the Mets, while Reardon went on to stardom in the Montreal bullpen.

The Mets, with the rest of baseball, suffered through the 1981 season, losing a third of their schedule to the strike. What was lost wasn't missed, as Torre's club posted an overall record of 41–62 for the split season, finishing fifth and then fourth. The lone bright spots were the performances of rookies Hubie Brooks (.307) and Mookie Wilson (.271 with 24 stolen bases), and some excellent relief work from Neil Allen.

It seemed a foregone conclusion that Torre would be gone after 1981, and he was, dismissed at the season's end. To replace him, Cashen reached back to an old Baltimore affiliate, George Bamberger. The fifty-seven-year-old Bamberger (like Torre, a New York native) was a highly regarded pitching coach for the Orioles when Cashen was in Baltimore, and later was a successful and extremely popular manager in Milwaukee. A heart attack had removed Bamberger from the dugout and he was working in the Milwaukee front office, fully recovered, when Cashen hired him.

In February 1982, the Mets finally made the kind of move they had been promising and the fans waiting for. They traded catcher Alex Trevino and pitchers Jim Kern and Greg Harris to Cincinnati for one of the league's premier big bonkers, George Foster. The deal was contingent on the Mets being able to sign Foster, a potential free agent after the '82 season. When the Mets offered George a massive five-year contract, rumored to be worth around $10 million, they had no trouble convincing him to come to New York.

On April 1, Cashen engineered one of the sweetest deals in Mets history. He traded the popular but increasingly less productive Lee Mazzilli to Texas for two minor-league right-handers, Ron Darling and Walt Terrell. Terrell was to be traded after a few years, but Darling, a highly resolved and tenacious competitor, was soon to develop into an ace pitcher.

Despite a fast start in 1982, the season ended with the Mets once again mired in last place. (Ironically, former skipper Joe Torre managed Atlanta to the Western Division title that year.) From June on, the club played poorly, with August being the worst month: their 5–24 record included a 15-game losing streak, tying the second-worst slump in club history.

Only Craig Swan (11–7) and reliever Neil Allen (19 saves in an injury-plagued year) did well on the mound. At bat, the heralded slugging duo of Kingman and Foster disappointed. While Kingman did lead the league with 37 home runs, they were largely nullified by 156 strikeouts and a .204 batting average. Foster, meanwhile, slumped to a .247 season with just 13 home runs, the worst outing of his career. The Mets did have a nonstop hustler in center field in Mookie Wilson, who batted .279 and set a club record with 58 stolen bases.

Nevertheless, 1982 was not a total washout for the Mets. In June, they had made another gilt-edged selection in the free agent draft. The selection's name this time was Dwight Gooden, a seventeen-year-old right-handed pitcher out of Tampa, Florida. Interestingly (and, in retrospect, amazingly) four other clubs, picking ahead of the Mets, passed over the youngster who, in two years, would become the National League's Rookie of the Year and in three years rise to truly spectacular heights.

In 1983, it was more of the same, last place again, but this time with a difference. The lights were at last beginning to go up on the Mets' horizon in what was going to prove a pivotal season. For one thing, the previous December the team had made an immensely popular move when they reacquired Tom Seaver from Cincinnati for pitcher Charlie Puleo and two minor leaguers. For the now thirty-eight-year-old "Tom Terrific" it was the fulfillment of a long-nurtured desire to come "home" (in more ways than one—he still lived an hour's drive from Shea), and to say that Mets fans applauded the move would be understatement.

In another move to satisfy Bamberger's desire for more pitching, Cashen acquired veteran right-hander Mike Torrez from the Red Sox. In addition, two young relievers had suddenly blossomed. In the right-left tandem of Doug Sisk and Jesse Orosco, the Mets were showing their best relief team since the days of Ron Taylor and Tug McGraw.

On June 15, right on the rim of the trading deadline, Cashen pulled a genuine coup. Swapping pitchers Neil Allen and Rick Ownbey to the Cardinals, he obtained in exchange first baseman Keith Hernandez. A former batting champion, co-MVP (with Willie Stargell in 1979), and Gold Glove fielder, Hernandez gave the Mets a dramatic infusion of high-style talent. From the moment he donned a New York uniform, the intense Hernandez became the on-the-field leader and catalyst the club had been missing. The grace and agility he brought to his work around the bag was as crowd-pleasing as any titanic home run launched by Kingman. But with the arrival of Hernandez, Kingman was sent to the bench, where he brooded and then sulked away the rest of the season, leaving behind a .198 batting average when the Mets released him the following January.

The New Yorkers had another new face in the outfield. Darryl Strawberry had joined the club soon after the opening of the season, and the tall, rangy youngster was soon to prove himself everything the scouts said he would be when they had urged him as the number-one draft pick. Strawberry was probably the finest all-around player ever to put on a Mets uniform. He could do each of the five basics required for greatness: hit, hit with power, run, throw, and field. The twenty-one-year-old youngster, who followed Seaver and Matlack in becoming a Mets Rookie of the Year, batted .257 and hit 26 home runs.

Foster, though hitting only .241, had come back with 28 home runs and 90 runs batted in. Hernandez, Strawberry, Foster, Wilson, Brooks: the Mets lineup had decisively shed its unoffending nature.

In the midst of all this, on June 3, Bamberger had resigned. Despite the rustling of talent arrived and on the way and the signs of better days nearing, "Bambi" could no longer contend with the frustrations of losing. The enticements of placid days at his home in Florida had finally become too seductive to resist, and George was gone.

Replacing Bamberger for the remainder of the 1983 season was his first-base coach, big Frank Howard, former long-baller for the Los Angeles Dodgers and Washington Senators, and long-proclaimed "baseball's strongest man." Howard worked hard and well, but the feeling was that a new man would be taking over in 1984.

There was a most positive feeling in the front office, despite the thud of another last-place finish. Some splendid ballplayers had collected on the roster—Hernandez, Strawberry, Brooks, Wilson, Foster. Veteran Rusty Staub had become a lethal pinch-hitter, at one point during the season setting a record with eight consecutive pinch hits. (Overall, the Mets tied a major-league record in 1983 with 12 pinch-hit home runs, four of them by Danny Heep.) The pitching was once again a bright spot, with a plethora of strong young arms. Orosco, Sisk, Terrell, and Darling were the kinds of pitchers you built a staff around. And down on the farm, at Lynchburg in the Carolina League, the Mets had that kid Gooden. All he'd done in 1983 was fan 300 in 191 innings.

Joe Torre. Joe played for the Mets from 1975 to 1977 and managed from 1977 through 1981. He batted .306 for the Mets in 1976.

John Stearns (1975–84). An excellent catcher and stubborn competitor, Stearns's career ended prematurely because of a shoulder injury. A .293 average in 1982 was his best.

Dave Kingman (1975–77, 1981–83). An all-or-nothing batter with a haymaker swing, Dave is the Mets' all-time home-run leader with 154. In 1982 he became the first Mets player to lead the league in homers with 37 (a club single-season record).

Jon Matlack.

Bob Apodaca (1973–77). Bob was a fine reliever for the Mets until arm trouble took him out of things. In 1975 he had a 1.48 ERA.

John Milner.

John Milner, coming home the hard way.

Mike Phillips (1975–77), utility infielder.

Dave Kingman.

Outfielder Del Unser (1975–76). Del batted .294 in 1975.

Jesus Alou (1975). The youngest of the three Alou brothers played sparingly for the Mets, batting .265.

Hank Webb (1972–76). Hank's only full season was 1975, when he was 7–6.

Outfielder Mike Vail (1975–77). In his rookie year Mike batted .302 and hit in a club-record-tying 23 straight games (broken by Hubie Brooks' 24 in 1984).

Third baseman Roy Staiger (1975–77).

American League veteran Mickey Lolich pitched just one year for the Mets (1976). The lefty was 8–13.

Accustomed to giving autographs, Dave Kingman is here on the receiving end. The signer is President Gerald Ford. The occasion is the 1976 All-Star Game in Philadelphia. At left is Commissioner Bowie Kuhn.

Skipper Joe Frazier on the phone to the bullpen. Joe managed the Mets in 1976 and part of 1977.

Bruce Boisclair (1974, 1976–79). An outfielder, Bruce had some good years at Shea, batting .287 in 1976, .293 the next year.

Hard-throwing right-hander Skip Lockwood (1975–79) was the Mets' chief fireman for several years. His best year was 1976 when he was 10–7, with 19 saves.

Ed Kranepool.

Jerry Koosman in 1978, his last year as a member of the Mets.

Doug Flynn (1977–81) had one of the snappiest second-base gloves in the National League.

Tim Foli, back with the Mets in 1978.

The flashy Willie Montanez (1978–79). He drove in 96 runs for the Mets in 1978.

Doug Flynn has just forced the Phillies' Greg Luzinski at second and is firing on for the double play.

Richie Hebner (1979), another third-base candidate. Richie did well, batting .268, but he wasn't happy in New York and moved on.

Alex Trevino (1978–81) caught and played several infield positions for the Mets.

Elliott Maddox (1978–80), outfielder and third baseman.

THE NEW YORK METS

In his two appearances against the Astros in the playoffs, Roger McDowell threw seven shutout innings.

Second baseman Tim Teufel slides safely into home.

Dwight Gooden and Gary Carter celebrate one of the Mets' 108 regular-season victories in 1986.

Darryl Strawberry watches his game-tying three-run home run sail out of the ballpark in the sixth inning of game 3 of the pennant playoffs.

Len Dykstra follows through on his game-winning two-run home run in the bottom of the ninth inning in game 3 of the playoffs.

Although his record was 0–1, Dwight Gooden pitched well against the Astros in the NLCS.

Dave Henderson brings home a run for the Sox at Fenway Park. Although the Mets took two of three games at Fenway, they still returned to Shea trailing in games 3–2.

Ron Darling opened the World Series for the Mets, losing a 1–0 heartbreaker on an unearned run.

Boston's Bill Buckner bangs out a hit at Shea, where the Mets fell behind two games to none.

Sid Fernandez, pitching in the shadow of Fenway's Green Monster, threw four shutout innings in a losing cause in game 5.

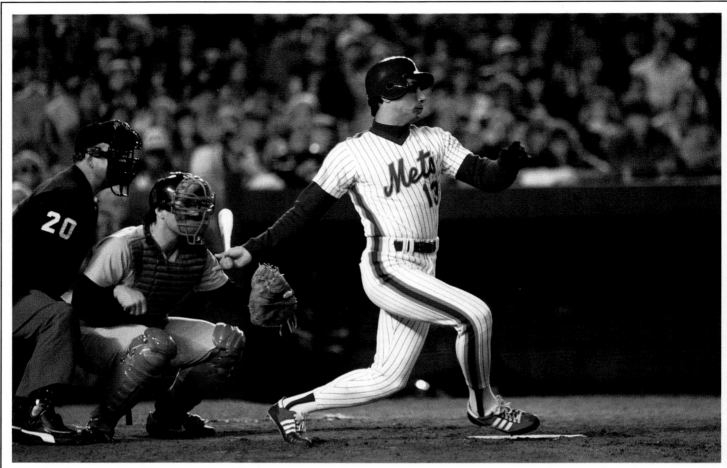

Lee Mazzilli delivered two crucial pinch-hit singles to start game-tying rallies in games 6 and 7.

Early in game 6 of the World Series, Keith Hernandez pounces on a bunt, fires to second base, and another sacrifice attempt is foiled.

Gary Carter tags out Jim Rice to choke off a Boston rally in the seventh inning of game 6.

Jesse Orosco earned three wins against the Astros. The superiority of the Mets' bullpen was a deciding factor against the Astros and Red Sox.

Mookie Wilson lies on the ground after leaping to avoid being hit by Bob Stanley's wild pitch in the bottom of the tenth inning of game 6. Kevin Mitchell raced home with the game-tying run.

Ray Knight jumps on home plate after Mookie Wilson's slow bouncer slipped between Bill Buckner's legs, allowing Knight to score the game-winning run in game 6.

Ray Knight leads off the bottom of the seventh inning of the final game with the home run that put the Mets ahead to stay.

Dykstra is welcomed by his teammates in the seventh inning of the final game after scoring the run that put the Mets up 5–3.

Gary Carter celebrates the final out of the 1986 World Series as strikeout-victim Marty Barrett heads for the dugout.

Jesse Orosco jumps for joy as the Mets become World Champions.

Left-hander Pete Falcone (1979–82). Pete threw well enough for the club to keep starting him, but the best he could show was 8–10 in 1982.

Right-handers Pat Zachry (*left*) and Craig Swan. Zachry (1977–82) both started and relieved for the Mets, with a 10–6 mark in 1978 his best showing. Swan (1973–84) had a career plagued with injuries. At his best, he was good enough to lead the league in ERA (2.43 in 1978).

Andy Hassler. The big left-hander worked in relief for the Mets in 1979, with a 4–5 record.

Frank Taveras (1979–81). Frank was the club's regular shortstop for three years. A singles hitter (he had just one home run for the Mets), he batted .279 in 1980.

Lenny Randle was the Mets third baseman in 1977–78. He batted .304 in '77, slumped to .233 the next year and was gone.

Lee Mazzilli (1976–81). Lee had some productive years with the Mets, the best being a .303 batting average in 1979.

The versatile Joel Youngblood (1977–82), who played second base, third base, and the outfield for the Mets. Seeing limited service in the 1981 strike season, he batted .350.

Steve Henderson (1977–80). Steve, a right-handed-hitting outfielder, had good years with the Mets, batting .297, .266, .306, and .290. He was traded to the Cubs in 1981 for Dave Kingman.

Nino Espinosa (1974–78). Nino's best was 10–13 in 1977.

Neil Allen (*left*) and Bob Apodaca. Neil (1979–83) was a Mets relief ace. Possessing a world of stuff, he never quite seemed to get the most out of it and was moved to St. Louis in the Keith Hernandez deal.

Claudell Washington. He played for the Mets for part of the 1980 season, batting .275, then left for Atlanta as a free agent.

Mark Bomback (1980). Mark was the Mets' top pitcher in 1980 with a 10–8 record, then was traded to Toronto for Charlie Puleo.

The Mets made a mistake when they let right-hander Jeff Reardon (1979–81) go to Montreal. Jeff pitched well in relief for the Mets, then became a star for the Expos.

Right-hander Ray Burris (1979–80).

Handyman Bob Bailor (1981–83) gave the Mets excellent service in both the infield and outfield.

Right-hander Charlie Puleo was 9–9 in 1982, then was traded to Cincinnati in the deal that brought Seaver back to the Mets.

Tom Hausman (1978–82). Shown here charting the pitches in that day's game, right-hander Tom Hausman was primarily a relief pitcher for the Mets.

Nelson Doubleday, chairman of the board of the New York Mets.

Fred Wilpon, president and chief executive officer of the New York Mets.

Frank Cashen.

Mike Scott (1979–82).

Walt Terrell (1982–84).

Frank Howard, who coached under Bamberger in 1982, then managed the team the last two-thirds of the 1983 season, after George resigned.

The former Cy Young Award winner with San Diego, Randy Jones (1981–82). By the time he reached New York, much of Randy's magic was gone.

Manager George Bamberger (*center*) posing with two dapper additions to his pitching staff, Tom Seaver (*left*) and Mike Torrez (*right*). Mike worked for the Mets in 1983, when he was 10–17, then was released early the next season.

Dwight Gooden.

RESURGENCE

DURING THE 1983 WORLD SERIES, Cashen announced the name of the new Mets manager. For Cashen, it was another "Baltimore connection." The new man was the Orioles' former second baseman Dave Johnson, in his prime a sharp-hitting, smooth-fielding player, and, even as a player, a keen student and observer of the game. More than once, Baltimore Manager Earl Weaver had found himself having to explain to an inquisitive Johnson the reasons and subtleties of certain strategic moves. "He always asked intelligent questions," Weaver recalled.

After working as an instructor in the Mets organization in 1982, Johnson had managed the number-one farm club at Tidewater in 1983, bringing the Tides in fourth but winning the championship in the playoffs. Bright, shrewd, intense, Johnson was a "new breed" skipper. Armed with a degree in mathematics, he employed a computer to help him in determining the relative strengths and weaknesses of his and opposing players. For Cashen, Johnson's appointment would prove an inspired choice.

When Johnson, professionally born and bred in the winning tradition of the Orioles, announced that his club would be a contender in 1984, skeptics wrote it off as the usual effusion from a new manager.

But before the 1984 season could begin, the Mets suffered a dismaying loss, both to their roster and from a public-relations vantage point. One of the results of the 1981 strike was the adoption of a new clause in the basic agreement between owners and players called "professional compensation." This allowed for a team losing a free agent in the reentry draft to select another player from a pool made available by most major-league clubs. One of the players left unprotected by the Mets was their thirty-nine-year-old future Hall of Fame pitcher, Tom Seaver. The club felt the need to protect as many of their young players as

possible; and they did not think anyone would choose the veteran pitcher because of his age and his weighty contract. They were wrong.

When the Chicago White Sox, on January 20, 1984, selected Seaver as their compensation pick (for the loss of pitcher Dennis Lamp to Toronto), the Mets and their fans were stunned. Frank Cashen was abashed, Tom Seaver was furious. The White Sox' reasoning was simple: despite his age and despite a 9–14 record in 1983, they felt that Tom Seaver was still Tom Seaver. (Chicago's acumen would be borne out in 1984: Seaver was their top pitcher with a 15–11 record.)

The loss of Seaver, according to baseball's deeper thinkers, would be a perhaps fatal blow to the Mets' hopes of breaking their lease on last place. And on the surface, there was some rationale for the thinking. For other than acquiring left-hander Sid Fernandez from the Dodgers over the winter, the Mets were relatively inactive in the off-season trade market. The club was going into spring training without any appreciable changes on the rooster.

But Dave Johnson knew something the skeptics didn't. That old Mets hallmark, young pitchers with strong, gifted arms, was never more in evidence. There was Ron Darling, with the speed of youth and the poise of experience. And Walt Terrell, a bulldog competitor with a hard, sinking fastball. And Ed Lynch, a versatile righty who could start or relieve. And young Fernandez, erratic, but with a world of stuff. And Orosco and Sisk in the pen.

But buzzing most insistently and captivatingly in the mind of Johnson was the name Dwight Gooden. Johnson had seen the youngster in the Mets' spring camp and been profoundly impressed. When his Tidewater club was going into the league playoffs, he had had the organization reach down to Lynchburg and elevate Gooden for the occasion. Dwight didn't disappoint: his two victories in three starts helped the Tides to the title.

Now it was the spring of '84. The Mets knew exactly what they had in the nineteen-year-old Gooden. But Cashen, a cautious type, was in favor of giving Dwight another year in the minors, at Tidewater; or at least start him off there and then promote him in midseason to the big team. Johnson argued that Dwight was ready right now. Johnson prevailed.

It was ironic, and perhaps symbolic, that the year Seaver left was the year Gooden arrived. For Mets fans it was a rebirth of the blazing splendor of Tom Seaver, and the analogy is hardly extravagant, for Gooden, in his first time around the big-league track, was to better Seaver's fine rookie season marks in wins, strikeouts, shutouts, and earned-run average.

And, like Seaver, Gooden immediately projected not just a mound dominance but a winning personality as well. Modest, unassuming, intensely competitive, the immensely likable youngster with the supreme inner confidence was youth and age at once: young in years, but in poise and self-discipline displaying a fully armed and mastered talent, magnetic enough to create an instant vogue—the "K" signs waved and aligned to demonstrate his strikeout prowess.

Talents of Gooden's dimensions come along so infrequently that they are like electric currents flashing through the wires of the baseball community. When he was making his very first start in the major leagues, in the Astrodome against Houston, Gooden heard that the Astros' Nolan Ryan, baseball's reigning strikeout king, was eager to see him pitch.

Johnson let his young starter go just five innings in that first start and Dwight came away with a 3–2 win. He was on his way.

And the Mets were on their way, too, to their most exciting season in a decade. With Gooden, Darling, and Terrell pitching well, and with Orosco and Sisk stalking in to hose down late-inning grass fires, the Mets found themselves in a pennant race.

Hernandez, Foster, Strawberry, Wilson, and Brooks were having good years. In addition, Johnson had installed at second base one of his personal favorites, Wally Backman. The fiery, switch-hitting Backman had been unable to impress previous Mets managers, but Johnson, who had managed Backman at Tidewater in '83, admired Wally's blood-and-guts style of play and insisted on playing him. Backman responded with a year of nonstop hustle and a .280 batting average.

Early in the season, the Mets made a gutty decision and resolved to go with their young pitchers and released veteran pitchers Mike Torrez, Dick Tidrow, and Craig Swan (eating some hefty contracts in the process). The midseason acquisition of right-hander Bruce Berenyi from the Reds gave Johnson the fourth starter he needed. At twenty-nine, Berenyi was the oldest pitcher on the staff.

The Mets played solid ball through the first half of the season, good enough to lead the division by 3½ games on July 26. But then the runner-up Cubs (managed by ex-Mets coach Jim Frey) came to town and took three of four. A week later the Mets went to Chicago and were swept in four games. They never regained their momentum, winning 90 games but finishing second, 6½ out.

Nevertheless, the season had been a turning point in Mets fortunes. The patient tinkering by Cashen, the blossoming of young players, and the skillful manipulating by Johnson had in one year turned the club around. And the fans were duly appreciative: attendance shot up by over 700,000, to over 1,800,000.

For Gooden it had been a year of records and spectacular performances. The Mets' fourth Rookie of the Year (and second in a row after Strawberry) broke Herb Score's major-league record for strikeouts by a rookie with a startling 276 (in 218 innings). He also established a new major-league record with 11.39 whiffs per nine innings (breaking the mark of 10.71 Sam McDowell set with Cleveland in 1965). On September 12 and 17, in back-to-back starts, he fanned 16 in each game, setting a new league record of 32 Ks in two consecutive games. From August 11 to the end of the season he was terrifyingly effective. In his last nine starts, covering 76 innings, the Mets phenomenon struck out 105, walked 13, and allowed just 42 hits. His final record was 17–9.

Darling, with a string of heartbreaking no-decisions in the second half, was 12–9. Terrell was 11–12, Berenyi 9–6, and Orosco 10–6 with 31 saves.

Hernandez led the hitters with a .311 batting

average, while Brooks hit .283 (including a club-record 24-game hitting streak), Wilson .276, while Foster and Strawberry each had power-laden years, George with 24 homers and 86 RBIs, Darryl with 26 homers and 97 RBIs. Rafael Santana, a late-season promotion from Tidewater, won the shortstop job, moving Brooks back to third after Johnson had experimented with Hubie at short. If the Mets had a soft spot, it was behind the plate. Cashen was determined to pave it over with some first-class concrete.

On December 7, 1984, Cashen surprised some people when he traded Terrell to the Detroit Tigers for third baseman Howard Johnson. With Brooks installed at third, and the veteran Ray Knight available, it seemed the switch-hitting Johnson was one third baseman too many. But Cashen was laying the groundwork for one of the most eye-opening deals in Mets history.

Three days later, the Mets and Montreal Expos took the sports headlines with a sensational five-man deal. New York sent four players to the Expos—Hubie Brooks, catcher Mike Fitzgerald, outfielder Herm Winningham, and pitcher Floyd Youmans, in exchange for the league's, and perhaps baseball's, premier catcher, Gary Carter.

Because Carter was being traded in the middle of a multiyear contract, it was within his right to demand a trade at the end of the year. In getting the catcher to waive this right, the Mets extended his contract and included a no-trade provision through the year 1989.

It was unusual for a player of Carter's stature to be offered in a trade. The Montreal reasoning for so doing was an exercise in convoluted logic, i.e., the personable Carter was not popular with his teammates because of his faultless public image; and though admittedly the team's best player, the Expos had never won a pennant with him. Well, if Carter's teammates had a problem with the always available and cooperative star, the problem lay with them. And if the Expos had never won a pennant with him, how did they expect to win one without him?

Montreal's creative logic was New York's gain, for in Gary Carter the Mets were getting one titan of a ballplayer—a catcher who could hit for average and with power, a man with unsurpassed defensive skills, a powerful throwing arm, an expert handler of pitchers, and overall a thoroughly positive influence on a ball club. In the parlance of the dugouts, Carter was a "gamer."

The Mets were now able to field the most potent lineup in their history, with the speed of Wilson and Backman at the top, followed by the snappy line drives of Hernandez and then the heavy artillery of Carter, Strawberry, and Foster.

With Brooks gone, Johnson planned to platoon Knight and Howard Johnson at third. The steady, dependable Santana was at shortstop.

On Opening Day, Carter paid his first dividend by slamming a 10th-inning home run to beat the Cardinals, the surprise team the Mets battled all season long, right down to the end. Injuries to their pitching staff soon took the defending division champion Cubs out of the race.

Along the way, the Mets put on one of their old-time, oddball marathon shows, a game that made the sports pages all over the country. It took place on the night of July 4, in Atlanta. After a long rain delay the game got under way and thereafter threatened never to end, by innings or by time. When the Mets edged into a 12–11 lead in the top of the 18th inning, the Braves had run completely out of players, except for a few starting pitchers.

Mets southpaw Tom Gorman got the first two outs in the bottom of the 18th. With no one left on the bench, Braves Manager Eddie Haas was forced to let pitcher Rick Camp come to the plate. Going into the 1985 season, Camp was a lifetime .062 hitter who had never hit a home run. Ahead on the count 0–2, Gorman got careless, or Camp got lucky. Rick drove a game-tying home run over the left-field fence, shocking everyone, most especially Camp. Baseball, that great game of heroic improbabilities and improbable heroes, had done it again.

In the top of the 19th, the Mets scored four runs. To protect the lead, they brought in a starting pitcher, Ron Darling. Ron ran into a bit of trouble but nailed it down, finally, 16–13. It was nearly four o'clock in the morning when it ended, with a few thousand fans staying on gamely for a promised fireworks display, which the weary Braves management was obligated to deliver.

It was a gripping, season-long pennant chase, one that kept interest in a high state of percolation all summer at Shea. Mets fans had never been treated to anything like this; the pennants in 1969 and 1973 had been taken on unexpected late-season surges. This time they were in it all the way, in first place as late as September 13, and never far from it after that.

As the nail-biting went on, it became apparent that a pair of three-game late-season sets with the Cardinals could be decisive. The first, at Shea, was taken by the Mets, two games to one. The loss was a heartbreaker—1–0 on Cesar Cedeño's 10th-inning homer off Orosco (after Gooden had pitched nine shutout innings).

When they went to Busch Stadium for three games, the Mets were in second place by just that—three games. A sweep would put them in a first-place tie with the season's final weekend coming up. With New York's WOR-TV, the Mets' television outlet, scoring record ratings for the games, the Mets took the opener 1–0 in 11, thanks to a sonic boom of a home run by Strawberry, and thanks to nine innings of classic shut-out pitching by Darling.

The following night Gooden moved the New Yorkers to within a game with his twenty-fourth victory of the season. But, desperately needing that final game to enter into a first-place tie with the Cardinals, the Mets came up short, 4–3. That was a Thursday night. On Saturday, the day before the season ended, the Cardinals clinched it.

As in any close-run pennant race, there were what-ifs. The biggest for the Mets in 1985 were: what if Strawberry had not torn ligaments in his thumb diving for a fly and been sidelined from May 11 to June 28, during which time the Mets went 20 and 23; what if Berenyi had not been out virtually the entire season with a bad shoulder; what if Wilson had not been lost for long periods with a bad arm?

As far as individual performances were concerned, Hernandez led the hitters with a .309 batting average and kept the instant-replay technicians busy all season long with his fielding gems. Carter, playing much of the season on aching knees, capped a strong season with 13 home runs in September (including three in one game against San Diego), batted .281, with 32 home runs and 100 RBIs. Strawberry batted .277 and, despite missing seven weeks, clubbed 29 home runs and drove in 79 runs. Foster hit 21 homers. Backman batted .273, Wilson .276.

The pitching was led by Gooden. The Mets had expected great things from their young ace, but maybe not this great, and surely not this soon. Dwight put up an astounding 24–4 record. Leading the league in wins, complete games (16), innings (276), strikeouts (268), ERA (1.53), and second in shutouts with 8, he was an easy Cy Young Award winner.

Behind Gooden was Darling with a 16–6 record, rookie Rick Aguilera with 10–7, Lynch 10–8, and Fernandez at 9–9. Sid fanned an impressive 180 in 170 innings, during which he yielded just 108 hits—an eye-catching statistic. It was a mixed year for Orosco, 8–6 with just 17 saves. But emerging unexpectedly was rookie right-hander Roger McDowell. Recovering from a bad elbow that had limited him to seven innings of minor-league work in 1984, the twenty-four-year-old sinkerball specialist made the club in spring training and, with Sisk hampered by injuries and ineffectiveness, emerged as a reliable late-inning stopper. He ended at 6–5 with 17 saves and a 2.83 ERA.

Overall, it was an exhilarating year. The Mets won 98 games, second highest total in their history (the 1969 world champions won 100). They tied their all-time run production with 695 (tying the 1970 club). Their 134 home runs were the most since 1962. For the first time they had three men with 20 or more homers in one season. Responding to all this, the fans came out, literally, in record numbers. The Mets' attendance of 2,719,547 was an all-time high for a New York baseball team.

A great year, and Mets fans could reasonably look forward to more and better. The team was a strong blend of youth and experience, speed and power, pitching and defense. With a fertile farm system, aggressive management in the front office, and a skilled and knowledgeable man in the dugout, the Mets and their fans could appraise the future with confidence and high expectations.

The keynote for that future was spoken by Dave Johnson at the end of the season. "I'm proud of my team," said the skipper. "I'm just not much for coming in second."

Dave Johnson.

Howard Johnson.

Hubie Brooks.

A beautiful summer's day at Shea, and hardly an empty seat in sight.

Mookie Wilson.

Rusty Staub, pinch-hitter deluxe.

Keith Hernandez.

Darryl Strawberry.

Wally Backman.

George Foster.

Lee Mazzilli.

Rick Aguilera.

Gary Carter.

Ron Darling.

Dave Magadan.

Randy Myers.

Danny Heep.

Roger McDowell.

Tom Gorman.

Terry Leach.

Len Dykstra.

Ed Lynch.

Sid Fernandez.

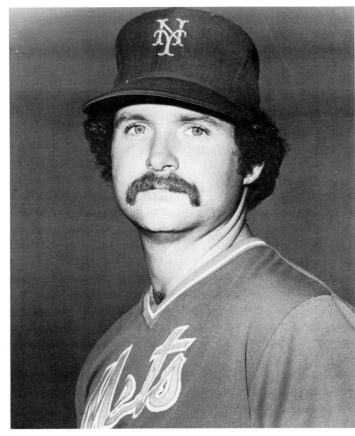

Terry Leach.

Doug Sisk.

Ron Gardenhire.

Dwight Gooden.

Clint Hurdle.

Television announcer Tim McCarver.

Television announcer Steve Zabriskie.

Radio announcer Gary Thorne.

Brent Gaff.

Gary Carter.

Keith Hernandez, ready to spring.

Jesse Orosco.

Rafael Santana.

Ray Knight.

Jesse Orosco.

Dwight Gooden.

Darryl Strawberry.

THE CUP RUNNETH OVER

There is inescapably in every spring camp a mood of optimism, born of the time of the year. A common description found in the sports pages to describe the quality of this ubiquitous buoyancy is "guarded." Baseball people as a rule are rather superstitious; to predict too grandly and with too inflexible a degree of certainty is to be considered pushy, if not arrogant, as well as downright risky. Nevertheless, believing they were going to win, many New York Mets said so, with Davey Johnson making the boldest utterance of all: "I don't want to just win the division; I want to dominate it." The quote was not overlooked in National League clubhouses. It was the most egregious gauntlet to be flashed around the league in a long time.

The optimism that prevailed in the Mets' 1986 spring training camp was solidly based, as far as the players were concerned. They believed they were the best team in their division, if not in the entire league. In addition, there was another deeply motivating factor: they were expected to win. They had come close in 1984, closer in 1985. There was a sense that if they did not get to the top this year they might never do it. Baseball history is replete with teams that have made strong second-place finishes for a couple of years, only to see their balloons burst and a precipitous drop through the standings ensue.

With some help from the wily Frank Cashen and some additional support from the farm system, Johnson's 98-game winners from 1985 were an even stronger team going into the 1986 season. Cashen had swung a trade with the Red Sox, obtaining left-hander Bob Ojeda and three minor-league pitchers for right-handers Wes Gardner and Calvin Schiraldi and outfielders John Christensen and LaSchelle Tarver, none of whom figured prominently in the Mets' immediate plans.

Ojeda had been little more than a .500 pitcher for Boston, but the Mets felt that his assortment of

breaking pitches, thrown with sharp control, would be more effective in Shea than they had been in Fenway with its neighborly left-field wall. (That he would end the season with the most wins and lowest earned-run average on a staff that included Dwight Gooden, Ron Darling, and Sid Fernandez was something totally unexpected.)

Another key addition was Kevin Mitchell, a right-handed-hitting product of the farm system. Mitchell, who could play infield and outfield (a versatility that became even more important as the big league clubs decided to go to war with 24-man rosters), caught Johnson's eye and won a job by dint of his solid hitting all through the spring.

Even one of the spring's most serious accidents had its positive side. After Mookie Wilson suffered a frightening eye injury when he was hit with a ball during a rundown drill, Johnson was forced to go with Len Dykstra in center field. Dykstra seized his wide-open opportunity and not only emerged as a top-of-the-lineup star, but his hustling, nose-in-the-dirt style of play made him a Shea favorite.

The Mets opened the season sluggishly, losing three of their first five games, but this was like a prehurricane doldrums, for the team was about to make one of the most blistering and highly sustained runs in National League history.

If one game in April, one game out of a schedule of 162, can be pointed to as a turning point, it was the one played in St. Louis on April 24. Playing for the first time in the home park of the team that had edged them out the year before and the team they considered to be their prime rival again in 1986, the Mets served notice, to the Cardinals and to the rest of the league, as to what kind of season it was going to be. The New Yorkers were losing the opener of a four-game series, 4–2, in the top of the ninth. Suddenly Howard Johnson blasted a stunning, game-tying two-run homer off the Cardinals' brilliant young reliever Todd Worrell. The Mets went on to win the game and to sweep the series.

Johnson's home run was at once dramatic and crucial and symbolic. Using the Cardinal sweep as the springboard for an 11-game win streak, the Mets finished April in first place with a 13–3 record and a five-game lead.

Many of the team's clutch hits were coming from a somewhat unexpected source—Ray Knight. Knight was trying to put together a season of redemption, having just experienced two highly disappointing, injury-plagued years. He was on the club in 1986 almost by default, and many were glad of it, most especially Davey Johnson, who had never lost faith in his veteran third baseman.

By the end of May, the Mets had won 31 of 43 games and were in first place by six games. Despite the loss of their projected number-three starter Bruce Berenyi to arm problems and the disabling of spot starter Ed Lynch (later dealt to the Cubs), the club's pitching was proving to be its strong suit. Dwight Gooden, Ron Darling, Sid Fernandez, and Bob Ojeda were the heart of the starting corps, backed by the league's best one-two bullpen combine, Jesse Orosco and Roger McDowell.

The club's sense of its own destiny filled it with a spirit that frequently boiled over into uncontainable enthusiasm. There was some grumbling from other teams that the Mets' high-fives, curtain calls (demanded by the Shea fans), and victory bear hugs displayed professional insensitivity and were "arrogant." But it was hardly arrogance; what was being demonstrated was a high-voltage winning chemistry, a terrific forward momentum that could not be contained, neither artistically nor emotionally.

The season was marred by several bench-clearing brawls, including a particularly ugly one with the Reds in Cincinnati on July 22, precipitated by Eric Davis's hard slide into Knight at third and Knight's clip of Davis with a right hand. This eventually turned into an extra-inning game and one of the season's most bizarre contests. Due to Johnson's earlier player moves and a couple of ejections after the brawl, Davey had to alternate Orosco and McDowell in right field and on the mound. The Mets eventually won the game in 14 innings, 6–3.

Moving with seemingly unstoppable force, the team swept through June with a 19–9 record, closing out the month with a 9½-game lead and 50–21 record, and showing no sign of slowing down. The team was so solid, in fact, that Cardinals manager Whitey Herzog, a hard-nosed realist, announced that nobody was going to catch the Mets. For an opposing manager to publicly throw in the towel so early in the season was a remarkable tribute.

Herzog turned out to be more correct in his observation than anyone realized. The Mets' first-place lead kept growing. At the All-Star break they were enjoying the biggest midseason lead built up by any National League team since the inception of divisional play in 1969—13 games.

Five Mets made the All-Star team—Darryl Strawberry, Keith Hernandez, Gary Carter, Dwight Gooden, and Sid Fernandez. Herzog, who selected the National League pitchers, might well have simplified his job and picked the entire Mets staff, for at the break Davey Johnson's aces had the following records: Fernandez 12–2, Gooden 10–4, Ojeda 10–2, and Darling 9–2. In addition, Orosco had 12 saves and McDowell 8.

The month of July had some checkered moments for the club. In addition to the Cincinnati brawl and another one in Atlanta (triggered when the Braves' David Palmer plunked Strawberry with a pitch after a Carter home run), four Mets had a run-in with the Houston police. Tim Teufel, Ron Darling, Rick Aguilera, and Bob Ojeda were celebrating the arrival of Teufel's first child after the game, when there was a confrontation with a couple of off-duty policemen working as security guards in a Houston nightclub. When the dust had settled, Darling and Teufel were hit with felony charges, Ojeda and Aguilera with lesser offenses, and all four had been hauled off to the stationhouse. The ultimate disposition of the charges was put off until early the following year. (In the end, it was a tempest in a teapot. Darling and Teufel each received a year's probation after pleading no contest to reduced charges, and the charges against Ojeda and Aguilera were dismissed. The probation was ended for the two Mets a month later.)

The Mets express continued rushing on its golden rails through August, winning 21 of 32 and inflating their lead to 19 games. During the month there was another unfortunate episode.

Soon after the All-Star break, Johnson had placed Dykstra permanently in center and platooned Mookie Wilson and Kevin Mitchell in left. With Strawberry a fixture in right, this made George Foster the odd man out. The veteran slugger, whose bat had slowed perceptibly, didn't like it. Early in August, Foster was quoted in a newspaper story as saying that black players were not promoted by the Mets as aggressively as white players (a statement with which no one came forward to agree). An angry Johnson requested his release and Cashen agreed, even though the club would have to eat the remainder of Foster's lucrative contract.

Replacing Foster on the roster was the Mets' one-time most popular player, Lee Mazzilli. Mazzilli had been signed as a free agent after having been released by the Pirates. Assigned to the Mets' Tidewater club in the International League, Mazzilli was there only a few days when Foster's release opened a roster spot for him. After his career had stagnated for five years with the Texas Rangers, New York Yankees, and Pittsburgh Pirates, Mazzilli was overjoyed to be "coming home," happily accepting his position as a role player. And he was a perfect fit—a switch-hitter with speed who could play first base and anywhere in the outfield.

After building to a lead of 22 games—the largest ever for a National League team since the beginning of divisional play—the Mets achieved the inevitable on September 17 at Shea when Gooden clinched the Eastern Division title with a 4–2 win over the Cubs.

In a replay of the victory-celebrating rampages of 1969, the fans poured onto the field and in a frenzy of joyous if mindless destruction caused severe damage to the playing field. Faced with a herculean challenge, the ground crew responded by working all night to get the field back into shape for the next day's afternoon game.

The Mets closed out the season with a record of 108–54 and a 21½-game lead over the second-place Phillies. Their victory total had been bettered only twice in National League history—by the Cubs' 116 in 1906 and the Pirates' 110 in 1909, and tied by the Cincinnati Reds in 1975.

Oddly, the club ended the season without a 20-game winner. Ojeda was the top winner with an 18–5 record, followed by Gooden's 17–6, Fernandez's 16–6, and Darling's 15–6. Rick Aguilera, who came on strong in the second half as the fifth starter, was 10–7. McDowell, tireless coming out of the pen all season (75 appearances), was 14–9 with 22 saves, while Orosco was 8–6 with 21 saves.

The Mets' spectacular season was reflected in the club's gaudy total attendance figure, 2,762,417. This set not only a new club record, but was also a new high for a team in New York City, in both instances the Mets extending their own record.

Interestingly for a team that won 108 games and was so dominant all season long, no Mets regular had a year that was statistically sensational. In fact, several key players had what might be described as subpar seasons. While Gary Carter knocked in 105 runs and hit 24 home runs, his batting average fell from 1985's .281 to .255. Darryl Strawberry drove in 93 runs, but saw his average drop from .277 to .259. Rafael Santana, a .257 hitter in 1985, slumped to .218, achieving that only with a good second-half spurt.

Keith Hernandez remained flawlessly consistent, following years of .311 and .309 with a 1986 batting average of .310, while maintaining his stunning defensive play at first base. For day-by-day followers of the team, Hernandez's intense involvement in the game and his hair-trigger intuitions became a compelling study in athletic concentration.

Among those who bettered their records in this memorable season were Mookie Wilson, rising from five successive years in the .270s to a career-high .289 average. Len Dykstra jumped from a .254 rookie season to .295. Ray Knight rose from the dregs of .218 in 1985 to a most productive .298, with 76 runs batted in. The most dramatic leap in personal fortune came from Wally Backman. The switch-hitting second baseman, a solid .273 man in 1985, shot up to a team-high .320 in 1986, a year that saw him doing considerable platooning with the right-handed-hitting Teufel.

Waiting for the Mets in the National league pennant playoffs were the Western Division winners, the Houston Astros. Under rookie manager Hal Lanier, the Astros had taken the West by 10 games. They had some solid citizens in third baseman Denny Walling, outfielder Kevin Bass (both .300 hitters), second baseman Bill Doran, veteran outfielder Jose Cruz, and first baseman Glenn Davis, the team's central power plant with 31 home runs and 101 runs batted in.

Houston's starting pitching was considered to be a match for the Mets'. Lanier's staff was topped by former Met Mike Scott. Scott had risen during the past two years from mediocrity to stardom, thanks to the development of a split-fingered fastball, a pitch that dropped suddenly and swerved sharply as it reached the plate, a pitch that Scott could deliver at 90 miles per hour. (There were some mutterings around the league that he also scuffed the ball occasionally, adding to its eccentric action.) Mastery of this pitch had turned Scott into a dominating pitcher. His 1986 figures were impressive: 18 wins (including a no-hitter) against 10 losses, and league-leading numbers in ERA (2.22) and strikeouts (306).

Behind Scott in the Astro rotation were lefty Bob Knepper (17–12) and another former Met, Nolan Ryan (12–8), at the age of thirty-eight still the possessor of a most formidable fastball, as his 194 strikeouts in 178 innings attested. Southpaw Jim Deshaies, with a 12–6 record, backed up Lanier's Big Three. The Houston bullpen was the primary responsibility of righthanders Dave Smith and Charlie Kerfeld.

The best-of-seven battle for the 1986 National League pennant began in Houston's Astrodome on October 8. The opposing pitchers were Dwight Gooden and Mike Scott. Billed as a pitchers' duel, the game proved to be just that. Gooden pitched brilliantly, but Scott was his match and just a bit more. In the bottom of the second inning, Glenn Davis led off for the Astros and tagged a Gooden pitch for a home run. It was the only run of the game, as Scott was positively overwhelming, fanning 14 and giving just five hits. Scott had been so masterful, in fact, that the thought of having to face him again later in the series was frankly disconcerting to many of the Mets' hitters.

The Mets drew even the following day. Bob Ojeda scattered ten hits while his teammates hammered out a solid 5–1 victory over Ryan. They did this with two quick bursts in the fourth and fifth innings. In the fourth, a double by Carter and a sacrifice fly by Strawberry drove in two runs; an inning later, a two-run triple by Hernandez keyed a three-run inning and sealed the win.

The series then traveled to Shea Stadium. Playing to more than 55,000 extremely vocal hometown fans, the Mets opened game 3 by falling behind 4–0 to Bob Knepper after two innings, the Astros taking advantage of a struggling Ron Darling. In the bottom of the sixth the Mets suddenly struck back with a game-tying four-run rally, the big blow being a rousing three-run homer by Strawberry. Hitting the home run off Knepper was particularly satisfying for Darryl, who had struggled all season against left-handers.

The Astros quickly untied the game against Rick Aguilera in the top of the seventh, scoring an unearned run with the help of a Ray Knight error.

The score stood at 5–4 going into the bottom of the ninth. The Mets had a man on base with one out. Pitching for Houston was their number-one reliever, Dave Smith. At bat was Len Dykstra, who had entered the game several innings earlier and remained in to play center field. Dykstra, who sometimes irked his manager by taking swings that Davey Johnson felt were out of proportion to his size, took one now. The youngster connected solidly and lined a high line drive over the right-field fence for the biggest hit of his young career—a two-run homer that gave the Mets an electrifying 6–5 victory and 2–1 advantage in games.

The following day, however, it was Scott again. With the Mets muttering that the Houston ace was scuffing the ball with sandpaper and the umpires saying he was not, Scott pitched another strong game, beating Fernandez and the Mets 3–1. Sid pitched tight ball, weakening only to throw a two-run homer to Alan Ashby in the second and a solo shot to Dickie Thon in the fifth. It was enough. The Mets finally broke through on Scott after 15 scoreless innings at his hands with a single run in the bottom of the eighth, but that was it.

Scott's three-hit, 3–1 victory tied the series at two games apiece. A glance into the immediate future told the Mets that if the series went to seven games the showdown would find them facing Scott. It was not a comfortable prospect.

The fifth game of the playoff series was one of the memorable games in Shea Stadium history. It was a duel of classic dimensions, both athletically and dramatically. The opposing pitchers were Houston's Nolan Ryan, the most prolific strikeout pitcher in history, and New York's ace, Dwight Gooden.

It was a heralded pitching matchup that fulfilled all expectations. Both hard-throwing right-handers were effective, Ryan superbly so. The Astros scored a run in the top of the fifth, but in the bottom of the inning the Mets came back to tie as Strawberry hit his second crucial home run of the series—this one a line drive to the right-field corner that was just inches fair and inches over the wall. Neither pitcher was to surrender another run. Ryan pitched nine innings, allowing one run, two hits, walking one and fanning 12. Gooden pitched the first 10 innings of the 1–1 tie (the first time in his big-league career he had gone past the ninth), giving up one run, nine hits, walking two and fanning four.

The game moved into the last of the 12th, still tied at one apiece. With Houston's Charlie Kerfeld on the mound (Orosco had come on for Gooden in the top of the 11th), Wally Backman singled. When Kerfeld erred on a pick-off attempt at first base, Backman went to second. Keith Hernandez was intentionally walked to fill the open base, bringing up Gary Carter. The Mets' cleanup hitter and big RBI man had been struggling in the series—one hit in 21 at-bats. "I knew it was just a matter of time," Carter said after the game. "I knew I was a better hitter than one for twenty-one." Indeed he was. Picking on a 3–2 pitch, Carter lined a low shot back through the box and into center field, scoring Backman with the winning run.

The 12-inning 2–1 win put the Mets up in games 3–2, with the series swinging back to Houston.

As game 6 got under way in Houston, the specter of Mike Scott began looming larger and larger, from the first inning on. In the bottom of the first the Astros jumped on Bob Ojeda for three runs. Thereafter, Ojeda and then Rick Aguilera pitched superbly through the eighth inning, holding the Astros in place. But Houston starter Bob Knepper was pitching a masterful game—shutout ball and just two hits over the first eight innings. The Mets' most recurrent nightmare—Mike Scott and his split-fingered fastball in game 7—was just three outs away from becoming reality. What happened in that top of the ninth, however, epitomized the Mets' entire 1986 season. That archetypical half

inning turned out to be a microcosm of the skill and resolution that went into the production of 108 regular-season victories.

Davey Johnson began the inning with one of his own remarkable flashes of judgment. Disdaining the righty-versus-lefty orthodoxy, he sent Len Dykstra up as a pinch-hitter against Knepper. Dykstra tripled (in a year of many significant hits, this was one of them). Mookie Wilson followed with a single into center, the ball just clearing the glove of the leaping Bill Doran. It was now 3–1.

After Kevin Mitchell grounded out, Hernandez doubled Wilson home, making it 3–2. That finished Knepper and brought on Dave Smith. Decidedly off his game today, Smith proceeded to walk Carter and Strawberry, loading the bases. Ray Knight then tied the game with a sacrifice fly.

Roger McDowell came on in the bottom of the ninth and went on to pitch five nearly flawless innings of shutout ball (the longest relief outing of his major-league career), allowing just one hit as one Astro batter after another mashed his hard-dropping sinker onto the ground.

The Mets broke the tie in the top of the 14th on a single by Wally Backman. Orosco took over in the bottom of the inning. With one out he gave up a home run to center fielder Billy Hatcher, tying the score, stunning the Mets, and sending thunderous waves of elation through the Astrodome.

The tiring Orosco got through the 15th, and then in the top of the 16th the Mets broke loose and scored three times. Strawberry led off with a pop-fly double. Knight, who had been knocking in crucial runs all year, did it again, bringing Strawberry in with a base hit. The Mets went on to make it 7–4, adding two more on a wild pitch and a one-bagger by Dykstra, who had remained in the game.

Down three runs, the gutty Astros were not about to fold. With one out, Orosco walked Davey Lopes and gave up singles to Doran and Hatcher, making it 7–5. Denny walling grounded into a force out. The Mets were one out away. But Glenn Davis dropped a single into short center to make it 7–6 and put the tying and winning runs on second and first. The next batter was Kevin Bass, a .311 hitter during the regular season.

Orosco was visibly tired, but Johnson had no intention of replacing him. His fastball having been popped around during the inning, Orosco threw nothing but breaking pitches to Bass, working the count to 3–2 before getting Bass to swing over a sharp, low-breaking bender for the final out.

After 4 hours and 42 minutes of intensely played baseball, the Mets had won the pennant—and avoided the unwanted seventh-game confrontation with Mike Scott.

It was a physically and emotionally drained Mets club that prepared to meet the Boston Red Sox in the World Series. John McNamara's club featured some solid hitters in third baseman Wade Boggs (the American League's leading hitter), first baseman Bill Buckner, catcher Rich Gedman, outfielders Jim Rice and Dwight Evans, and designated hitter Don Baylor, who under newly instituted rules would be in the lineup only during games in the American League home park.

Boston pitching, traditionally the team's weak point, was anchored this year by the fireballing Roger Clemens, 1986's premier pitcher with a 24–4 record. Along with Clemens were southpaw Bruce Hurst, righty Dennis (Oil Can) Boyd, and relief pitchers Bob Stanley and ex-Met Calvin Schiraldi. Schiraldi, obtained in the Bob Ojeda deal, had joined the Sox in midseason and became the strong man of the Red Sox pen.

Missing the Series because of a knee injury, and thus depriving the Series of what would have been pure drama, was Boston's fourth starter, the forty-one-year-old former Met ace Tom Seaver. Seaver had been acquired by Boston earlier in the season from the Chicago White Sox and pitched well for the Red Sox.

The Series opened at Shea on the night of October 18, with Hurst opposing Darling. It was a tense pitchers' duel through six scoreless innings. In the top of the seventh the Red Sox broke the deadlock with an unearned run, scored when Teufel let a ground ball skip through his legs. That was the game, a skillful 1–0 win for Hurst (with a ninth-inning save for Schiraldi), a heartbreaking loss for Darling.

In game 2, the match was Gooden vs. Clemens, a shootout between two of the game's most charismatic young fastballers. To the surprise of almost everyone, however, the two aces were gone by the sixth inning. The Red Sox peppered Gooden steadily, reaching him for eight hits and six runs in

five innings. The Mets had meanwhile disposed of Clemens in the bottom of the fifth, and at the end of that inning the score was 6–3, Boston. The final was Boston by 9–3.

The two teams then took the short journey to Boston to play games 3, 4, and, if necessary, 5 at old Fenway Park. With an off day intervening, the word "wall" was a featured part of almost every newspaper story. Down two games to none, the Mets had "their backs to the wall"; and how would their hitters, fielders, and pitchers cope with The Wall, Fenway's fabled "Green Monster" in left field, whose height and neighborliness made batters eager, pitchers (especially lefties) nervous, and left-fielders anxious.

Wall or no wall, Johnson started Ojeda in game 3, reasoning that the lefty, who had pitched for several years in Fenway, would not be intimidated. Davey was right. Ojeda worked a smooth seven innings before giving way to McDowell. Together, the two combined on an easy 7–1 win, built mainly on a four-run first inning. Len Dykstra had started the game with a home run off Oil Can Boyd. This was followed by singles by Backman and Hernandez, and then a Carter double, a rundown play that was botched by the Boston infield, and a two-run single by Danny Heep. The rest of the game was a Mets script.

The Mets evened the Series with a second Fenway victory the following night. Darling started against Al Nipper and again pitched well, this time receiving some support from his teammates. The Mets broke a scoreless game open with three runs in the top of the fourth, two scoring on a Gary Carter home run, the third on a Knight single.

In the top of the seventh, Dykstra poled his second homer of the series, a two-run shot that deflected off the glove of a leaping Dwight Evans in right field. In the eighth, Carter belted another one out, high over the wall in left and into the Boston night. The final score was 6–2, Mets, with Darling going seven scoreless innings and Orosco picking up a shaky McDowell in the last of the eighth.

In game 5, the final one at Fenway, Bruce Hurst returned for the Sox, facing Gooden. Hurst was again strong, scattering ten hits (including a Teufel home run) in a 4–2 Boston win. Gooden gave up all the Boston runs and nine hits in four-plus innings. After having pitched so superbly against Houston in the playoff series, the Mets' young ace had disappointed twice in the Series. Relieving Gooden in the fifth, Sid Fernandez, relegated to long relief in the Series, pitched airtight ball for four innings, fanning five.

The teams returned to Shea for game 6 and, if necessary, game 7. The Red Sox were now one game away from their first world championship since 1918. Three times since then—in 1946 and 1967 against the Cardinals and 1975 against the Reds—the Sox had taken a World Series to a seventh game and lost. Sixty-eight years without a world title (along with several blown pennants) had convinced many of Boston's history-minded fans that the club was laboring under a hex.

According to one whimsical interpretation of the Red Sox' misfortunes, the club had brought down a curse upon itself when in 1920 it had sold baseball's one undisputed deity (Babe Ruth) to the city of Sodom and Gomorrah (New York). The facetious logic of the theory aside, a fatalistic hardcore of Boston's colorful legion of fans, from Maine fishermen to account executives of Fairfield County, from taciturn Vermonters to garrulous Boston cab drivers, from New Hampshire innkeepers to Cambridge dons, were convinced, in a mix of philosophies and superstitions, that their beloved team was jinxed. If supportive evidence was called for, they had history, and then suddenly they had game 6.

Through the first five games it had been a fairly routine World Series. In each of the games, the team that scored first had won without ever relinquishing the lead. But as game 6 of the 1975 Series had been so unforgettable (with Boston winning that one on Carlton Fisk's resounding 12th-inning home run, only to lose it all the next day), so game 6 would make the 1986 World Series one to sparkle in memory's center.

The Sox started out well in game 6, nicking Bob Ojeda for runs in the first and second innings, while a blazing Roger Clemens fanned four.

At the end of four innings it was still 2–0, with Clemens pitching scoreless, hitless ball, and whiffing six. Then, in the last of the fifth, the Mets tied it. The runs came in on a Strawberry walk, a stolen base, an RBI single by Knight, a Mookie Wilson single, and a double play hit into by Heep.

The Sox broke the tie in the top of the seventh, scoring an unearned run off McDowell that was keyed by Knight's throwing error. (At that moment Knight was being measured for goat's horns. One game later he would be voted the Series' Most Valuable Player, so quickly do the fates spin in baseball.)

The Mets tied it in the bottom of the eighth, picking on their old teammate Schiraldi, who had just replaced Clemens. Lee Mazzilli led off the inning with a pinch single. When Schiraldi picked up Dykstra's sacrifice bunt and bounced a throw to second trying to get Mazzilli, both runners were safe. Backman bunted them along, Hernandez was walked to fill the bases and Carter came up. Schiraldi worked the count to 3–0 and Johnson gave Carter the green light. Gary lined a hard sacrifice fly to Rice in left and the game was tied.

The tie lasted until the top of the 10th, when the Sox unloaded on Rick Aguilera. Dave Henderson homered, making it 4–3. The Sox scored another run and took a 5–3 lead into the bottom of the 10th, three outs away from their first World Series win in 68 years.

Wally Backman flied out to left, and the Sox were two outs away.

Keith Hernandez flied to center, and the Sox were one out away.

The Red Sox were poised on their dugout steps, waiting for Schiraldi to get that last out and begin the celebration that would embrace all of New England.

But there was a bump in the road, named Gary Carter. Whacking a 2–1 pitch to left for a single, Carter kept the game alive. And then another bump in the road, this one named Kevin Mitchell. Batting for Aguilera, the Mets' young rookie handyman lined an 0–1 pitch to center for another single, sending Carter to second.

Ray Knight was the next bump in the road, and again Schiraldi could get neither around nor over it. Behind 0–2, Knight dropped a one-bagger into short center, scoring Carter and sending Mitchell spinning around to third with the tying run.

At this point, McNamara replaced Schiraldi with the veteran Bob Stanley. The batter was Mookie Wilson. The count went to 2–2. Wilson fouled off the next two pitches. Stanley then delivered a pitch that suddenly took on a life of its own. "It was an inside fastball," an unhappy Stanley said later, "that was supposed to tail back out over the plate." Instead, the ball tailed sharply in and down on Mookie, who leaped into the air and seemed to hang suspended there for a moment with his legs folded under him while catcher Rich Gedman dove frantically to his right to try and intercept the ball. The ball got by him and shot all the way to the screen while a joyous Mitchell roared home with the tying run.

The wild pitch sent Knight to second. After fouling off two 3–2 pitches, Wilson unfurled a three-bouncer down to first baseman Bill Buckner, a Series sub-hero for playing on tired and battered ankles that wobbled when he tried to run. Buckner waited for the ball, the inning-ending out. The last bounce, however, was an irregular one and carried this peculiarly Mets-loving baseball—this baseball that was defying intents, purposes, and now almost inevitability itself—under Buckner's glove and into short right field where it rolled with its final assertion of perverse independence while Ray Knight came tearing around third with the winning run, culminating the most incredible rally in World Series history.

The Series was tied at three games apiece, and Red Sox fans wondered if their hearts were going to be broken yet again. They were given an extra day to ponder the caprices of that rogue baseball while the rains poured upon Shea Stadium, causing a one-day postponement of game 7.

The opposing pitchers in game 7 were each making their third start of the Series, Bruce Hurst for Boston, Ron Darling for New York.

The Sox started well, longballing Darling early. In the top of the third Dwight Evans and Rich Gedman slammed homers, Wade Boggs drove in a later run with a single and it was 3–0. The score and the inning—3–0, Boston, after three—carried eerie echoes for New England fatalists, for it reflected precisely the situation of game 7 in 1975, which the Sox had gone on to lose to the Reds.

Sid Fernandez relieved Darling in the fourth and turned in a pivotal performance. The hard-throwing lefty burned away the Red Sox batters through the sixth inning, fanning four and keeping his team in the game.

In the bottom of the sixth, the Mets got to a weakening Hurst. Another vital pinch-hit by Mazzilli started it, followed by Wilson's single and Teufel's walk to fill the bags. Keith Hernandez banged a two-run single and a few moments later, Backman, running for Teufel, scored the tying run on an odd right-field-to-second-base force out.

In the bottom of the seventh, with Hurst gone, the Mets pounced on an acknowledged Red Sox deficiency—their bullpen. Ray Knight's lead-off homer against Schiraldi made it 4–3, Mets. Hits by Dykstra and Rafael Santana and Hernandez's sac fly made it 6–3.

The Red Sox fought back in the top of the eighth, scoring two and tightening it to 6–5. In the last of the eighth, Strawberry launched a cannon shot that made it 7–5. Another run scored later when Orosco, expected to bunt, surprised everyone by swinging away and surprised them even more by punching an RBI single through the Boston defense, making it 8–5.

Orosco breezed through the top of the ninth, fanning Marty Barrett (ironically, the Series star with a record-tying 13 hits) for the final out.

It was over.

Across a 162-game season and then 13 post-season games one looks back at those special signposts and symbols that delineate a team's character. Because of the significance of the occasion, two episodes stand out with particular clarity. The team's death-defying rally in the bottom of the 10th inning of game 6 was one that will live forever in World Series history and in the annals of the Mets. That rally and the storming of the Houston portals in the ninth inning of the sixth game of the pennant playoffs were the Mets' remarkable season in miniature. Those resolute comebacks stand as spokesmen for a season of 108 regular-season wins and eight more under baseball's most grueling pressure.

The dream that had begun in spring training was now a memory to savor through the coming winter and for the years to follow. In the year of their silver anniversay, the twenty-fifth season of their exciting and unpredictable adventures, the New York Mets had won their third pennant and their second world championship. Their millions of fans had bestowed the gift of loyalty; the team had responded with the gift of victory.

Bob Ojeda.

San Diego's slugging outfielder Kevin McReynolds, acquired in a December 1986 deal for Kevin Mitchell and several minor leaguers.

Kevin Mitchell.

Dave Magadan.

An exultant Len Dykstra rounds the bases after his game-winning two-run homer in the bottom of the ninth inning beat Houston in game 3 of the pennant playoff.

Keith Hernandez has just connected for a triple in the fifth inning of the second game of the Houston playoff series. The blow knocked in two runs.

Darryl Strawberry watching the flight of his game-tying home run off Nolan Ryan in the bottom of the fifth inning in game 5 against Houston.

A study in contrasts: A dejected Charlie Kerfeld walks off the field as behind him the Mets rush to celebrate Gary Carter's game-winning hit that gave them a 12-inning 2–1 victory in game 5 against Houston.

Dwight Gooden getting a champagne shower in the clubhouse after the Houston clinching.

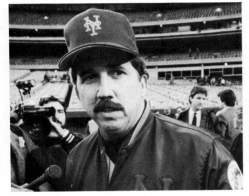

Davey Johnson being interviewed on the field at Shea prior to game 1 of the World Series.

Len Dykstra pinch-hitting his crucial triple off Bob Knepper in the top of the ninth inning of game 6 at Houston. The hit launched a game-tying three-run rally.

The Mets have just clinched the pennant in Houston, and Len Dykstra is leaping upon his joyous teammates.

Ron Darling at work against the Red Sox in game 1 of the 1986 World Series.

Dwight Gooden about to unload against the Red Sox in the first inning of game 2.

It's the top of the seventh inning of game 4 at Fenway Park and Len Dykstra has just belted a Steve Crawford pitch for a home run. The catcher is Rich Gedman, the umpire Joe Brinkman.

This is Dykstra's home run ball, just bouncing off the glove of Red Sox right fielder Dwight Evans.

Game 6 of the 1986 World Series ended on a bizarre note; it also began on one as a visitor from outer space dropped in on the Shea Stadium proceedings in the top of the first inning. The visitor was quickly escorted into official custody.

Gary Carter is right on that Steve Crawford delivery in the top of the eighth of game 4 at Fenway. Gary rode it out for his second homer of the game. Catcher Rich Gedman and umpire Joe Brinkman are eyewitnesses.

Bob Ojeda reaching back in the first inning of game 6.

Ron Darling pitching in the top of the first inning of game 7 at Shea.

Mookie Wilson leaping away from the Bob Stanley wild pitch that tied game 6 in the last of the 10th inning.

The elation of the moment is plainly on the faces of coach Bud Harrelson (left) and Ray Knight as Knight carries across the winning run on Bill Buckner's error in the bottom of the 10th inning of game 6.

It's the bottom of the eighth inning of game 7 at Shea, and at the instant this picture was taken the Mets were leading 6–5; but Darryl Strawberry is about to land on this Al Nipper pitch and punch it out for a 7–5 Mets lead.

Len Dykstra applauds himself across the plate, scoring on Rafael Santana's single in the bottom of the seventh in game 7. Catcher Rich Gedman is less than thrilled. The umpire is John Kibler.

The moment of victory. A triumphant Gary Carter is clutching the last pitch of the 1986 World Series—Jesse Orosco's strikeout of Marty Barrett (*left*).

Carter (*right*) is about to bound into the beginning of the Mets victory celebration.

THE NEW YORK METS: YEAR BY YEAR

YEAR	WON-LOST	POSITION	MANAGER
1962	40–120	Tenth	Stengel
1963	51–111	Tenth	Stengel
1964	53–109	Tenth	Stengel
1965	50–112	Tenth	Stengel-Westrum
1966	66–95	Ninth	Westrum
1967	61–101	Tenth	Westrum-Parker
1968	73–89	Ninth	Hodges
1969	100–62	First	Hodges
1970	83–79	Third	Hodges
1971	83–79	Third (tie)	Hodges
1972	83–73	Third	Berra
1973	82–79	First	Berra
1974	71–91	Fifth	Berra
1975	82–80	Third (tie)	Berra-McMillan
1976	86–76	Third	Frazier
1977	64–98	Sixth	Frazier-Torre
1978	66–96	Sixth	Torre
1979	63–99	Sixth	Torre
1980	67–95	Fifth	Torre
1981	41–62	Fifth/Fourth*	Torre
1982	65–97	Sixth	Bamberger
1983	68–94	Sixth	Bamberger-Howard
1984	90–72	Second	Johnson
1985	98–64	Second	Johnson
1986	108–54	First	Johnson

NOTE: Division play began in 1969.   *Denotes split season.

METS TEAM LEADERS: YEAR BY YEAR

YEAR	BATTING AVERAGE*	HOME RUNS	RUNS BATTED IN
1962	Mantilla, .275	Thomas, 34	Thomas, 94
1963	Hunt, .272	Hickman, 17	Thomas, 60
1964	Hunt, .303	C. Smith, 20	Christopher, 76
1965	Kranepool, .253	Swoboda, 19	C. Smith, 62
1966	Hunt, .288	Kranepool, 16	Boyer, 61
1967	Davis, .302	Davis, 16	Davis, 73

YEAR	BATTING AVERAGE*	HOME RUNS	RUNS BATTED IN
1968	Jones, .297	Charles, 15	Swoboda, 59
1969	Jones, .340	Agee, 26	Agee, 76
1970	Agee, .286	Agee, 24	Clendenon, 97
1971	Jones, .319	Agee, 14	Jones, 69
		Jones, 14	
		Kranepool, 14	
1972	Staub, .293	Milner, 17	Jones, 52
1973	Millan, .290	Milner, 23	Staub, 76
1974	Jones, .282	Milner, 20	Staub, 78
1975	Unser, .294	Kingman, 36	Staub, 105
1976	Millan, .282	Kingman, 37	Kingman, 86
1977	Randle, .304	Henderson, 12	Henderson, 65
		Milner, 12	
		Stearns, 12	
1978	Mazzilli, .273	Montanez, 17	Montanez, 96
1979	Mazzilli, .303	Youngblood, 16	Hebner, 79
			Mazzilli, 79
1980	Henderson, .290	Mazzilli, 16	Mazzilli, 76
1981	Brooks, .307	Kingman, 22	Kingman, 59
1982	Wilson, .279	Kingman, 37	Kingman, 99
1983	Wilson, .276	Foster, 28	Foster, 90
1984	Hernandez, .311	Strawberry, 26	Strawberry, 97
1985	Hernandez, .309	Carter, 32	Carter, 100
1986	Hernandez, .310	Strawberry, 27	Carter, 105

*Based on 502 plate appearances, except 1981 (326 plate appearances).

YEAR	WINS	STRIKEOUTS	EARNED-RUN AVERAGE
1962	Craig, 10	Craig, 118	Jackson, 4.40
		Jackson, 118	
1963	Jackson, 13	Jackson, 142	Willey, 3.10
1964	Jackson, 11	Stallard, 118	Cisco, 3.61
1965	Fisher, 8	Jackson, 120	Fisher, 3.93
	Jackson, 8		
1966	Fisher, 11	Fisher, 127	Ribant, 3.21
	Ribant, 11		
	Shaw, 11		
1967	Seaver, 16	Seaver, 170	Seaver, 2.76
1968	Koosman, 19	Seaver, 205	Koosman, 2.08
1969	Seaver, 25	Seaver, 208	Seaver, 2.21
1970	Seaver, 18	Seaver, 283	Seaver, 2.81

YEAR	WINS	STRIKEOUTS	EARNED-RUN AVERAGE
1971	Seaver, 20	Seaver, 289	Seaver, 1.76
1972	Seaver, 21	Seaver, 249	Matlack, 2.32
1973	Seaver, 19	Seaver, 251	Seaver, 2.08
1974	Koosman, 15	Seaver, 201	Matlack, 2.41
1975	Seaver, 22	Seaver, 243	Seaver, 2.38
1976	Koosman, 21	Seaver, 235	Seaver, 2.59
1977	Espinosa, 10	Koosman, 192	Espinosa, 3.42
1978	Espinosa, 11	Koosman, 160	Swan, 2.43
1979	Swan, 14	Swan, 145	Swan, 3.30
1980	Bomback, 10	Falcone, 109	Zachry, 3.00
1981	Allen, 7	Zachry, 76	Scott, 3.90
	Zachry, 7		
1982	Swan, 11	Falcone, 101	Swan, 3.35
1983	Orosco, 13	Seaver, 135	Seaver, 3.55
1984	Gooden, 17	Gooden, 276	Gooden, 2.60
1985	Gooden, 24	Gooden, 268	Gooden, 1.53
1986	Ojeda, 18	Gooden, 200	Ojeda, 2.57
		Fernandez, 200	

INDEX